Touching Tomorrow
The Emily Griffith Story

Touching Tomorrow
The Emily Griffith Story

Debra Faulkner

*To Laurie
With warm regards
Debra Faulkner*

Filter Press, LLC
Palmer Lake, Colorado

To my mother, Laurel,
the teacher who touches all my tomorrows.

ISBN-13: 978-0-865410-78-7
ISBN-10: 0-865410-78X
Library of Congress Control Number: 2006920182

Filter Press, LLC
P.O. Box 95
Palmer Lake, CO 80133

Manufactured in the United States of America

Contents

Foreword

mong Colorado history's colorful cast of characters, perhaps the most admirable—and enigmatic—is a tiny, selfless, energetic schoolteacher named Emily Griffith. Though she may have told a little white lie or two about her age, Miss Griffith told the truth about Colorado's need to reform public education. Concerned about at-risk children, she realized that the key to their success or failure was the parents. So she opened up one of America's first free public schools "for all who wish to learn," where adults of any age could learn English and job skills. Even more remarkably, she did this at a time when the Ku Klux Klan ruled Colorado and pushed very different ideas about how to treat poor foreigners and people of color.

Emily Griffith's Opportunity School, which now occupies an entire city block in downtown Denver, has given hundreds of thousands a better life. Yet her own life ended in a bizarre murder still unresolved.

Emily's full and astonishing story is told here for the first time by another gifted teacher. Debra Faulkner first became interested in Emily Griffith in my Colorado history course at the University of Colorado at Denver. Assigned to select, research, and portray a prominent citizen interred in Denver's Fairmount Cemetery, Faulkner chose Griffith because she had worked with similar student populations in adult education classes she taught. Faulkner found that Emily's Opportunity School had been offering the same innovative programs—such as adult remediation, English as a Second Language, and vocational classes—since 1916. She became enamored with learning more about the visionary woman who started it all.

For five years, Debra Faulkner immersed herself in the search for the full details of Emily Griffith's life and death. By delving into contemporary newspapers and periodicals, as well as the archives of the Opportunity School and the Denver Kiwanis Club, Faulkner has created a more complete record than previous Griffith biographers.

Touching Tomorrow: The Emily Griffith Story also chronicles Griffith's shocking murder and the investigation surrounding it with unprecedented thoroughness and detail—even interviewing the last surviving Boulder County sheriff's officer to work on the case. Faulkner suggests in these pages a new theory of who-done-it and why.

Faulkner's diligent digging has revealed much about this incredible woman who not only took care of Denver's uneducated masses, but also cared throughout her life for a developmentally disabled sister. At a time when Americans are once again struggling with high dropout rates and what to do with the many foreigners flocking in to our country, this biography is more than just crackerjack history. This is a polished and thoughtful tale with a lesson for the present and the future. It revives a woman whose life's work represents one of the best and most inspiring chapters in the history of the peoples of Colorado.

Tom "Dr. Colorado" Noel
Professor of History
University of Colorado at Denver

Preface

Something was wrong. Ethel Gurtner knew it beyond doubt the morning of June 19, 1947, when she heard the plaintive barks of Chips, her sisters' cocker spaniel, apparently left outside all night. Ethel had banged on the locked door, even the windows of the neighboring cabin. Why didn't Florence and Emily answer? She'd hurried back to the Pinecliffe service station for her husband, Evans, and the key. Now she hovered at his back, anxiously wringing her age-spotted hands as he fumbled with the lock.

Evans cracked open the door and called out. Except for the babbling rush of South Boulder Creek nearby and the chirping of birds, they heard not a rustle, not a breath. He pushed the door open, stepped across the threshold, turned toward the bedroom, and stopped. Another step and he would have tripped over the body.

His sister-in-law Emily lay dead on the floor, shot in the back of the head and left face down in a pool of blood. Florence was found in the other bedroom, also shot through the back of the skull, apparently while kneeling with her hands behind her back.

Within 24 hours, headlines across Colorado and the nation decried the shocking slaying of Miss Emily Griffith, world-renowned educator and founder of Denver's famous Opportunity School. To the thousands who had known her or known of her work, the tragedy offended decency and defied explanation.

Boulder County sheriff's officers arrived on the scene to hear the distraught Ethel explain that she and Evans had spent the previous day in Denver. They had returned home to the little canyon resort of Pinecliffe in early evening, and she'd walked up to her sisters' cabin to visit before bedtime. When her knock brought no response, she assumed they'd gone out for a twilight stroll along the creek or through the woods, as they sometimes did. It was not until the next morning that she became alarmed.

Investigators found no signs of a struggle or forced entry. All the windows were locked from the inside. The single door latched automatically behind anyone who left the cabin.

In the rustic kitchen, two pots of food—mashed potatoes and baked beans—sat on a sideboard, apparently removed from the stove minutes before the murders. Three slices of apple pie were served on plates, one piece substantially larger than the other two. By all appearances, the elderly sisters had been expecting a guest for dinner.

Reporters nosed about, snapping photos of the crime scene and the bloodstained floor. As the investigation wore on, dark clouds gathered and thunder reverberated up and down the narrow canyon. Law enforcement officials interrogated every Pinecliffe resident and visitor who came to gawk and gasp. With whom did the victims associate? When were they last seen? Who could have wished these harmless old ladies dead?

Villager after villager mentioned the name of Fred Lundy. He was the Griffith sisters' closest friend. He'd helped them out with odd jobs for years, chopping firewood, buying groceries, driving them on errands. He was known to share meals with them. Regularly. And the things he'd been heard to say lately, everyone concurred, were all looking suddenly suspicious.

But where was Fred Lundy now?

1
Headwaters

The man approaching the canal dock was mildly surprised to encounter three children waiting there. A gangly boy of about thirteen perched atop a pylon, whistling as he whittled. His younger sisters sat facing each other, tossing jacks on the uneven planking. The man carried a copy of Mark Twain's *Tom Sawyer*. He looked toward the canal barge tied to the pier for the night, as if awaiting a signal. The older girl looked up with interest.

At the end of the dock, the children's father and their uncle, the boat's operator, emerged from the cabin, laughing and shaking hands. The boatman put his arm around Andrew Griffith's shoulders, told him it was good to see him and his brood, and asked after the health of his wife and youngest daughter.

When at last Griffith hobbled up the dock to rejoin his children, the man with the book shook his hand, then excused himself and headed for the docked boat. Darkness was quickly deepening the dusk. The boatman lit a bright lantern, which hung outside his cabin door. It illuminated a sign beneath, written in bold, hand-painted letters. The older girl stopped twirling jacks and read the words aloud. "For All Who Wish to Learn."[1] She looked at that sign for quite some time.

Why, she wondered, did her uncle want to be a teacher? He already had a job with his Erie Canal barge. Did grown-ups pay him a lot for their lessons? The foreign-looking man with his secondhand *Tom Sawyer* did not appear to have much money. Did her uncle help them simply out of the goodness of his heart because they had nowhere else to go to learn?

Young Emily Griffith had never pondered such things before. But she was profoundly impressed with the importance of what was being offered so selflessly. After considering it all awhile longer, a very practical question occurred to her: If people couldn't read, how would they know what the sign said?

Emily gazed down the path, where another man and his wife, each carrying a book, walked toward the floating night school, hand in hand, smiling hopefully. Suddenly, the simple truth became obvious—Folks just needed to see the light.

———

Though the Colorado governor and legislature later decreed otherwise, Emily K. Griffith entered the world not long after the American Civil War. Her Cincinnati birthplace made her an Ohioan. The February 10 date made her an Aquarius. And the Griffith family's Scottish ancestry made her a lifelong Presbyterian.

The eldest daughter of Andrew and Martha Griffith, Emily had a brother, Charles, two years her senior. Three years after Emily, Florence was born.[2] A second brother, Wallace, died in infancy.[3] Martha, described as frail and an invalid, delivered Ethelyn (also called Ethel) when Emily was eight.

Though charming and eloquent by all accounts, Andrew Griffith struggled in his trained profession. As a lawyer, he found his Calvinist conscience often at odds with the letter of the law, refusing to take a case if he did not believe his prospective client to be entirely in the right. Confusing the law with actual justice may well have doomed him in the legal profession.

Andrew abandoned his law practice at the age of forty-seven and thereafter became an itinerant missionary. Crippled and lame, he limped about with his one-horse cart, peddling Bibles and religious tracts. While noble, it was not a particularly lucrative enterprise. The family floundered financially and moved frequently.

During these formative years, the Griffith children attended Kirby Road and Central Ward schools in Cincinnati. Their education was repeatedly disrupted by the family's relocations, and, as a result, their elementary studies were inconsistent at best.

Florence struggled the most with school. Emily's sister was poorly equipped to deal with academia. Today's educators would probably describe her challenge as a learning disability. In the 1870s, teachers called her "feeble minded," and insensitive classmates doubtless called her worse. From childhood on, Emily assumed the role of Florence's defender and protector, appreciating as few did her sister's good heart and generous spirit.

Throughout their Cincinnati years, Emily and her siblings were surrounded by diversity and change. Ohio's industrial growth, initially stimulated by the Civil War, was eclipsing diversified agriculture in the nation's third most populous state. The ethnic character of the state changed, too. The black population grew threefold in the quarter century following the withdrawal of the Wyandot Indians in 1843.

Forty percent of Cincinnati's inhabitants were foreign born. Recently transplanted Germans, Serbs, English, Scots, and Irish comprised the largest ethnic groups. No doubt there were plenty in need of Emily's uncle's free night classes, which included English language lessons.

The city of Cincinnati had grown up near the confluence of the Miami and Ohio rivers. Floods were prevalent in those days, and residents were used to the ebb and flow, the rise and fall, of times and tides. Accustomed though they were to disasters, even Cincinnatians were caught off guard by the national financial scandal of 1884. Although the country in general had prospered, the railroads were suffering from declining profits due to rate wars, overbuilding, and mismanagement. When the brokerage firm of Grant and Ward closed, a Wall Street panic ensued. One in ten businesses failed, and foreign investors began to withdraw gold. In addition to the decline in railroad construction and lower steel prices, the complex reasons for the panic included protective tariffs, a series of iron workers' strikes, and bad loan decisions by several national banks. The reactionary wave of selling passed quickly and left the underlying economy essentially intact. But before it was over, economic ripples spread throughout the nation's manufacturing centers, sending their citizens, including Cincinnatians, scrambling for higher ground. Many chose to bail out altogether.

Andrew Griffith, too, registered the subtle economic backwash, as apprehensive neighbors, suddenly obliged to choose between their daily bread and the Good Book, invariably chose bread. Eventually the Griffith family, like so much social flotsam and jetsam of the mid-1800s, drifted downstream toward the promise of the western plains.

Prairie homesteading in the nineteenth century called for hardy souls. But not all who answered that call fit the profile. Andrew Griffith walked with a limp, and he had trained as a lawyer, not a farmer. But Griffith was not one to be deterred from the dogged pursuit of a dream. His daughter Emily inherited the same tenacious optimism, which would serve her well throughout her life.

In the spring of 1884, Andrew filed claim on 100 acres in Arnold Precinct, Custer County, Nebraska. His wife's poor health rendered her of little use in proving up the homestead. His second daughter, Florence, suffered debilitating bouts of epilepsy. Little Ethelyn, all of eight years old, could perform only light and simple tasks. Andrew became a justice of the peace, paid on a piecework basis for issuing legal papers and performing "marryin's and buryin's." But his income was small and sporadic. Any missionary funds he might have hoped for from the Presbyterians back home were diverted to disaster relief with the 1884 summer flooding of the Ohio Valley.

It fell to eighteen-year-old Charles and sixteen-year-old Emily to help support the family. Charles managed to secure a position as post-master in the little hamlet of Milldale (now extinct), the nearest town to the Griffith claim. Milldale lay between the settlements of Calloway and Arnold, four miles to the northwest. Emily, having finally completed the eighth grade in Overton, saw teaching as the only acceptable option for employment.

The three-member Custer County school board faced a chronic problem in those days. No sooner did they hire and train a school-teacher than she was lured away by a proposal of marriage. The turnover was frequent and disruptive, and they were forced to consider all candidates, regardless of age or experience.

Miss Emily Griffith, looking even younger than her sixteen years, struck the board as too naïve and vulnerable to assume responsibility for a classroom. Nonetheless, as desperate men taking desperate measures, they put her to the test. The first ordeal involved simple mathematical computations, which she completed with ease. The spelling challenge was met with equal success. She read beautifully. She knew her U.S. history and the capitals of all the states.

At last, she was directed to write something on the chalkboard so that the school board could judge her penmanship. Two members, quite satisfied with the results, nodded their approval. But the third scowled, declaring categorically that he disapproved of the way the young applicant wrote her *s*'s. Determined to impress and charm him as she had the other gentlemen, Emily smiled sweetly and reshaped the letters to suit her examiner's taste.[4] Even then, she understood the value of making small concessions to achieve greater goals.

Upon completing and passing "normal training," the two-week course required to earn a teaching certificate, Emily Griffith was hired and assigned to a sod schoolhouse on the Nebraska prairie. The ages of her students ranged from six to twenty-six. The petite schoolmarm was half the size of some of her older male pupils. To stay ahead of her more advanced students, she often studied late into the evenings.

Emily left no photographs or papers of her "soddie" years, but accounts by her contemporaries offer a representative picture of the experience. On the whole, schoolhouse conditions were miserable. Classrooms were supplied with a table and chair, benches for the students, and a box of chalk. Blackboards were a luxury. Often a sheet of building paper treated with lampblack served as a makeshift substitute.

Harper's Reader, The Spencerian Copy Book, Harvey's Grammar, Ray's Arithmetic, and the *McGuffy Speller* were standard texts. *Mitchell's Geography* and *Barnes History of the U.S.* were considered optional. Students began at the level suitable for their needs and progressed through the schoolbooks at their own pace.

Most of the primitive facilities had wood-burning stoves, but wood was far too precious a commodity to burn in this place where habitable structures were built of sod. Coal, too, was prohibitively pricey, owing to freight costs. So on bitter cold days, twists of hay, corncobs, or cow chips were fed into the stove. During blizzards, snow blew through the walls. The straw used to insulate the dirt floor was a breeding ground for fleas. Though the vermin must have made concentrating on studies more challenging, constant scratching had the unexpected benefit of keeping students awake and active.[5]

With infinite patience and diligence, prairie schoolmarms peeled ice-caked wraps and mittens from their frozen charges on wintry mornings, and layered them back on before launching them into the drifts for miles-long expeditions homeward. Weather was a continual source of challenge and complaint on the prairie, where homesteaders battled not only blizzards, but also scorching droughts. One of the few stories from this time that Emily Griffith was known to share drew its drama from a tornado.

She had lived in Nebraska long enough to recognize the signs of an approaching twister. Emily spotted those very signs one afternoon as she diligently drilled her pupils on their multiplication tables. She was teaching in a one-room frame schoolhouse that stood alone on the vast expanse of undulating plains. The storm came up suddenly, assaulting the building with angry gusts and pelting the single window with rain. The sky grew black, then dark green. No cellar or nearby gully offered a safe place to herd the children. She could hear what sounded like a locomotive approaching.

The children looked to her, anxious and afraid. The young teacher kept her composure and, with calm authority, directed her charges to line up, straight down the center of the room. As the ominous roar from outside grew louder, she ordered them all to hold hands and challenged them to drown out the sounds of the wind by singing hymns at the top of their voices.

They continued singing as the tornado hit the flimsy structure full force. It lifted the roof, and all four walls collapsed into the vacuum. But when it had passed, the center supports stood firm, as did the strategically placed string of children, clinging to one another and to their teacher.[6]

It was this sort of pluck, courage, and level-headedness that won the devotion of Emily's students and their families. Because prairie schools were isolated amidst far-flung homesteads and often distant from towns, the custom in those days required teachers to "board around," spending a fortnight at a time living with the families of their pupils, an arrangement for which they were charged $7 monthly out of their $25 salary. Most homes were devoid of comfort. The teacher sometimes shared a bed with two or three family members, partook of abysmal meals, and tolerated livestock in the living quarters. Like it or not, they became part of the intimate family of of their students.

Emily Griffith did like it. Described as having a friendly and sunny disposition, she loved people and was beloved by them. They were naturally drawn to her and sought her out when they were in need or in trouble. Upon occasion, the teenaged schoolmarm even had to steel herself for a crash course in midwifery, helping with the home delivery of a baby if no one else was available.

On the 1880s frontier, three out of five Nebraska homesteaders were foreign born or the first-generation descendants of immigrants. They were Germans, Swedes, Bohemians, and Norwegians who had come to America seeking better lives. It quickly became apparent to young Emily that these hopeful newcomers might never realize their aspirations for improved prospects without knowing basic English. How could they communicate with their new neighbors, with shopkeepers or officials, if they did not speak the language? How could they handle day-to-day transactions, keep up with news that affected them, or help their children with their lessons if they did not read English?

Though she spoke nothing but English herself, Emily did her best to help the immigrant families with whom she boarded, teaching them English phrases and explaining local customs. But such efforts made only the slightest dent in the language problem.

Even among the native English-speaking families of her pupils, many parents lacked fundamental academic skills. Often, families with whom she boarded asked her to read from the Bible at night, or to check the bill from the general store to be sure they had been fairly charged. The young teacher was dismayed at how many adults could not read or write or perform even the simplest computations. The rates of school attendance and grade school completion in the latter half of the nine-teenth century were low by today's standards. Struggling parents often pulled their children out of school, relying upon them to help with the family farm or business or to supplement the household income with menial jobs outside the home. In 1880, 17 percent of the U.S. popula-tion fourteen years and older was illiterate, with a higher rate among the foreign born.[7] As adults lacking a childhood education, where could these people go to learn the things they had missed?

Emily Griffith's frustration grew steadily throughout these years. She began to resolve to create a place where people of any age could be instructed in the skills they needed to succeed in daily life. In the nine-teenth century, this was a radical concept. Public education was for the young—and the young *only*. The sole purpose of schools was to teach children the three Rs.

Emily took a different view. The primary aim of education, she believed, was to prepare people for meaningful work and a productive place in the community. This definition applied, she reasoned, to folks of any age or background. Learning should be a lifelong process, open to "all who wish to learn," exactly as the sign on her uncle's barge had promised.

As the years passed, Emily taught near Westerville, then at the Tuckerville School, alternating between "soddies" and frame school-houses. In 1889, she was invited to teach third grade in Broken Bow's new seven-room, all-brick grade school, the showpiece of the county. Around that same time, her 23-year-old brother Charles married Minnie Shaw, 20, of Milldale. Justice of the Peace Andrew Griffith presided at the ceremony. From thence forth, Charles had his own family to support.

Pretty, blue-eyed Emily, too, had her share of romantic prospects. From schoolboys to sodbusters, many were smitten, but few were taken seriously. She may have considered, but never accepted, proposals of marriage. Financial support of the family weighed heavily upon her slight shoulders, and Emily was the sort to place others' needs above her own. As biographer Yale Huffman speculated, "Broken romance deflected Emily's loving nature toward her charges."[8]

Despite the 1888 decline in grain prices, the Andrew Griffith family, against all odds, perfected the patent on their homestead. Final receipt to the place came on Christmas Eve. For a brief time, the future looked bright.

The following autumn, Emily brought the Griffith family clock to school, where it was used not only for classes, but also for the weekly Grange meetings and Sunday school groups that met in the building. Never could she have anticipated the barbaric events her simple need for punctuality would precipitate.

Soon after the clock's installation, it was brazenly pilfered. Indignant, two local school board members, Hiram Roten and William Ashley, pursued the culprit—an easy task, since wagon tracks led directly from the school to the thief's house. When confronted by the gentlemen intent upon recovering the timepiece, Albert E. Haunstine confessed and handed it over. But as the board members walked away, Haunstine took down his rifle and shot them both in the back.

He fled, after taking $40, a rifle, a revolver, and the watches off the bodies of his victims. He was apprehended, tried, and convicted soon thereafter. An appeal, followed by a sanity hearing and temporary reprieve, bought Haunstine a two-year delay in execution. Threats of mob justice finally led to his hanging in the Broken Bow courthouse yard on May 23, 1891.

To the two thousand assembled for the grim spectacle, Haunstine offered a scaffold apology for the trouble and expense he'd caused the county. Sheriff J. B. Jones hanged him nonetheless. For the two murders he'd committed, the perpetrator was "jerked to Jesus" not once, but twice.[9]

It was enough to make a gentle soul such as Emily reconsider a life on the wild frontier.

2
Confluence

Nebraska homesteaders in the latter half of the nineteenth century braved prairie fires, plagues of grasshoppers, droughts, downpours, and plummeting agricultural prices. In May 1894, an unusually late hard freeze nipped crops in the bud. The "furnace winds" that swept across the already devastated plains that summer were the final straw for many. Settlers surrendered in large numbers, often abandoning claims and moving away with the few belongings that remained to them.

As the main provider for the Griffith clan, Emily had a substantial say in what was to become of the family. The idea of endless struggle against the elements held no appeal, and incidents such as the lynching of the clock thief undoubtedly soured her on the primitive frontier. What bright young woman wouldn't begin to long for a place more civilized, a place with more people and greater potential?

Exactly how or why the Griffith family settled on Denver as their new Jerusalem is unknown. Perhaps they knew someone who had moved to the "Queen City of the Plains" earlier. Maybe it was the allure of the majestic Rocky Mountains. It may have been because of depressed real estate prices in the wake of the 1893 Silver Crash that had devastated Colorado's economy. It is even conceivable that Emily was attracted by the progressive attitude evidenced by the second state to grant its women the right to vote.

Regardless of the motivations, in the autumn of 1894, the Griffiths arrived in Denver with Andrew's one-horse cart and their meager possessions. With disappointing proceeds from the sale of the homestead, they purchased a modest house on Lipon Street, between 12th and 13th avenues.

The family didn't remain at that address long. During their early years in Denver, the Griffith residence changed almost as often as Andrew's occupation. He switched from lawyer to itinerant missionary and back again as the mood struck him.[1] Once again, it was Emily who had to earn a steady paycheck to keep the household going.

It is difficult from a twenty-first-century perspective to comprehend the stigma once attached to the feminine condition known as spinsterhood. In the late Victorian era, any passably attractive young woman in her twenties who remained unmarried was thought to be deficient in some way. That she might actually choose to forego matrimony was inconceivable.

Thus Emily Griffith, applying to the Denver Public School (DPS) system at the age of twenty-seven, faced a choice. She could forthrightly report her circumstances and endure the condemnatory appraisal reserved for "old maids" of the 1890s. Or she could use this opportunity to start anew, with a few inconvenient details modified.

DPS records from 1895 reveal that Miss Emily Griffith reported her date of birth to be February 10, 1880. As easily as that, she neatly shaved twelve years off her actual age and was suddenly revitalized as a fifteen-year-old.[2] Petite and round-faced, she had always looked younger than her years; now age and appearance were more closely matched. Emily held to her little white lie until the day she died.

It was not until the 1980s that her lifelong misrepresentation came to light when biographer Yale Huffman looked into Ohio and Nebraska census records. Ohio records from 1880 revealed that Andrew Griffith listed his daughter Emily's age as twelve; in the 1885 Nebraska census, the eldest Griffith girl was seventeen. Both documents support an actual birth date of 1868, prompting the question: Who would have been more likely to misrepresent her age—her father or Miss Emily herself? Recently, historian and author Joyce Lohse banished any confusion about the harmless deception by locating Ohio census records for 1870, which list Emily K. Griffith, age two.

Her rejuvenation was not without its price. A fifteen-year-old Emily could believably claim no more than ten months' teaching experience, although in truth, she had taught for nearly ten years. Her fabrication led to the well-known characterization of young Emily as a fourteen-year-old prairie schoolteacher, an appealing myth she herself perpetuated.

The Denver School Board was not about to put one so young and inexperienced in full charge of a classroom. Emily was hired as an alternate, or substitute, teacher. Only three years later, after completing the training at Denver Normal School required for teacher certification, was she granted a teaching assignment of her own at the Central School in the Auraria neighborhood. By 1898, one of the world's most visionary educators had concluded all the formal training she would ever undertake.

It was probably at Normal School that she first encountered Fordyce Cleaves, a dashing young instructor of forensics (public speaking), recently employed by the Denver Conservatory and College of Music. After a period of ardent courtship, Emily accepted Cleaves' proposal of marriage. In 1903, he established the Cleaves School of Expression in a downtown office building, and he expected his betrothed to teach there with him once they were wed.

The many ways in which Cleaves resembled her father initially attracted Emily. But as the relationship became more serious, these very similarities may well have worried her. Biographer Yale Huffman observed, "Like Andrew Griffith, Cleaves relied upon his persuasive eloquence for a living, and she feared he offered little promise as a steady provider."[3] Who better to recognize that hard truth than a daughter who had supported her father's family since the age of sixteen? Cleaves' scattered employment history demonstrated to Emily an instability of character. His assumption that his future wife should simply sublimate her career ambitions to his goals did not sit well either. Emily was formulating plans of her own.

It is unknown exactly when and why Emily Griffith conceived the idea of a school open day and night, where people of all ages could come whenever it fit their schedules, to learn whatever it might be that could make their lives better. Her dream grew, and she spoke of it every chance she got to anyone who would listen. This school would teach English for the foreign born and what was in that day called "Americanization" for aspiring citizens. Remedial and literacy classes would be offered for those who, for whatever reason, had missed out on reading and writing and figuring when they were young.

The school she envisioned would also be a place to learn a craft or a trade, enabling students and their parents to make a better living for themselves and their families. She believed that such a school could—and must—be created. Intuitively recognizing the value of branding, Emily came up with a memorable name for this new sort of school early on. It was Opportunity.

Cleaves, like most middle-class men of his time, might have failed to see merit in his fiancé's reformist ambitions and taken them less than seriously. But the real problem probably came with his ultimatum regarding Emily's younger sister. Less able than most to cope with life's complexities, Florence would be dependent upon her sister their entire lives. She suffered from a learning disability unrecognized and unnamed at the turn of the twentieth century. She was often mis-understood and marginalized by those who did not know and love her. Fearing the treatment she might face without his sheltering protection, their father extracted Emily's solemn pledge before he died that she would never allow Florence to be institutionalized.

Fordyce Cleaves tested that promise. He wanted to marry Emily. But he had no intention of taking on the care of her simple-minded younger sister. He beseeched Emily to entrust Florence's welfare to others, or the marriage was off. The dilemma was difficult, but Emily's decision was never in question. Upon breaking their engagement, Cleaves seemed to disappear from Denver. In 1914, he died alone in San Francisco.

In addition to Cleaves, biographer Elinor Bluemel referred to what "was perhaps the one real romance in her life"—a dashing and well-to-do military officer who courted Emily ardently, showering her with gifts and amorous attention for years. According to Bluemel, Emily continually resisted any suggestion of more intimate commitment, protesting that her obligations to the support of her family precluded any consideration of matrimony.[4] Her reason, however, seems spurious in light of the fact that the gentleman reportedly pledged time and again his willingness to relieve her of that burden by providing for the entire Griffith family if she would but allow him. One is left to wonder what was actually behind her repeated refusals.

The city of Denver, not yet fifty years old, had grown from a slapped-together gold rush settlement at the confluence of Cherry Creek and the South Platte River to a relatively respectable metropolitan center of nearly 130,000 by 1895. Indians and bow-legged cowpokes could still be seen loitering about the lower downtown streets, as could gamblers, roustabouts, teamsters, and prostitutes.

Uptown, sharing a bluff with the unfinished state capitol, millionaires presided over ostentatious mansions, and the "Sacred Thirty-Six"—an elitist group of socialites—resolutely barred the nouveau riche Margaret Tobin Brown (later known as "Unsinkable Molly") from their ranks.

At the northwest end of 17th Street, Union Station had been the gateway to and from Denver since determined boosters—not to be daunted by the Union Pacific Railroad's bypass through Cheyenne— had raced to connect Denver to the transcontinental railroad via the Denver Pacific Railroad in 1870. The depot's massive, inescapable clock tower had synchronized the city, and the sleepy cow town had never been the same since.

By 1895, Denver had six daily newspapers, thirty-seven weeklies, and twenty-two monthlies. Downtown boasted impressive buildings: the Kittredge Building, the Masonic Building, the Equitable Building, the Mining Exchange, the Oxford and Brown Palace Hotels, and the no-expense-spared Tabor Office Block and Tabor Opera House.

On Denver's west side, the families of Emily Griffith's Central School pupils lived in modest, even shabby abodes, clinging to the lower rungs of the socioeconomic ladder. Those lucky enough to find employment supplied the unskilled labor sustaining smelters and slaughterhouses, laundries and liveries, stockyards and rail yards.

Years of "boarding around" in students' homes on the Nebraska prairie had impressed Emily with how family life affected children's academic performance. Disturbed by the high incidence of truancy in her classes, she began to investigate the home circumstances of the frequently absent pupils. What she discovered disturbed her even more. In many cases, her sixth-graders were missing school because their labors were needed to help their families subsist. They worked as newsboys, maids, cook's helpers, or telegram deliverers for a few cents a day. But their families counted on every penny.

Emily did what she could for the students and their families, often using her meager personal funds to help them buy groceries, medicines, or clothing. She called them her "folks" and took an almost maternal interest in their welfare. One young immigrant boy remembered, "She was always smiling at you and ready to take you by the hand. And when her hand touched yours, you knew she had great sincerity and a warm heart."[5] With a sense of humor, unusual likability and selflessness, she earned the friendship and trust of people of all ages and backgrounds. She was known as a good neighbor, there to help. Folks took to her.

Her promotion to eighth-grade teacher a few years later placed her in a part of town even more impoverished. Twenty-fourth Street School, in the Five Points neighborhood east of downtown Denver, needed a good disciplinarian as much as it needed a unique humanitarian. Griffith proved to be both.

When she looked up truant students after hours in this neighborhood, she found desperation, despair, ignorance, hunger, alcoholism, domestic violence, and crime. These underprivileged people, racial minorities, and non-English-speaking newcomers were sometimes trapped in demoralizing and demeaning situations, with little chance of improving their lot and escaping a downward spiral.

Emily Griffith saw a way out. She realized that poverty was the result of their problems, not the cause.[6] The root of the evil was a dirth not only of money, but of hope. Emily knew the truth of the maxim that knowledge is power, or more precisely, empowerment. Education could provide the tools to chisel promising futures from even the stoniest situations.

She began to offer, on her own time and for no remuneration, classes for the parents and working children among her Twenty-fourth Street folks during lunch hours and in the evenings. She taught arithmetic and reading, and English for immigrants. The night classes were a special challenge, as the school had no electric lights. Undaunted learners brought their own lanterns. What the dedicated teacher offered was precious, and her pupils devoured it gratefully, recognizing the potential to widen employment and advancement prospects substantially by mastering basic skills. Her caring attitude and selfless efforts earned Emily the nickname "The Little Mother of the Twenty-fourth Street School."

The Five Points neighborhood was ethnically and racially diverse, encompassing African Americans, Chinese, Hispanics, Italians, Japanese, Jews, and Native Americans, along with other minority groups. Children from thirty-seven different nationalities attended the school at 24th and Market streets durring these years. Emily treated all with compassion, dignity, and respect. Her liberal embrace was atypical for the time and place. A few years earlier, Colorado had passed a law legalizing segregated schools. Governor Albert McIntire decreed that no Catholic could hold any state office or job. Inclusion was an unknown concept in turn-of-the-century Denver. But to Emily Griffith, it came naturally.

Education officials took note of her extraordinary dedication to her pupils and her natural teaching ability and concluded with perverse bureaucratic logic that she belonged elsewhere. In 1904, Emily Griffith accepted their offer of an administrative position and found herself installed in the capitol as deputy state superintendent of schools under Superintendent Katherine L. Craig.

The Colorado State capitol occupied a world entirely removed from Five Points. The glorious granite structure, begun in 1886, was still under construction. The dome that rose 180 feet from the center of the Corinthian, cross-shaped edifice was not yet gilded. No expense had been spared on this monument, with floors of Colorado Yule marble and interior walls paneled in rare rose onyx. The gleaming bronze railings throughout all three floors were imported from Emily's home state of Ohio. At the official dedication on July 4, 1890, Governor Job A. Cooper had declared the building "worthy the Centennial State, a palladium of liberties and emblem of knowledge." The fourteenth step to the west entrance had been adjudged by Denver University scholars to be situated at 5,280 feet—precisely one mile—above sea level.[7]

Five-foot-two Emily Griffith must have felt even smaller as she entered the capitol and turned the doorknob, embossed with the state seal, to her office. But she soon proved herself more than equal to the assignment. In her deputy superintendent position, the quintessential schoolmarm entered a broader, more powerful new realm. She met and mingled with the influential players in the Colorado Department of Education and learned how things got done. To every school administrator with whom she came in contact in her official capacity, Emily expressed her concern for "the misunderstood pupil who fell under the disinterest of a thoughtless teacher"[8] and pupils bereft of the basic necessities of life.

Throughout her four years as a state administrator, Emily never lost touch with her former pupils or their families. An office stenographer from that period recalled many a barefoot and ragged youngster who found his way to Miss Griffith's new workplace. Sometimes they came simply to visit. Often they came seeking her help with some family or school crisis. When needed, she went without hesitation—in the middle of the day if circumstances so dictated—to fetch groceries for the needy family of a widowed woman taken ill, to retrieve an intemperate father or older brother from the local saloon, to mind the baby of an unwed mother while she sought work. Emily was a pragmatist. She addressed the immediate needs of others, without passing judgment—then reflected on ways to alleviate the underlying problems.

Time and again, her compassionate analysis led to the same conclusion. Education was the key, to improved prospects, to greater opportunity, and, most important, to hope. It was the way out and the way up for the underprivileged. She was increasingly determined to make her dream of free public education for people of all ages and circumstances a reality.

After four years in the capitol, Emily chose to return to the classroom teaching she so sorely missed. The night classes she'd initiated for the fathers and mothers of the children she taught by day resumed, and once again, she did what she could to make a difference in their lives. In January 1909, Miss Emily Griffith was awarded a complimentary state teaching diploma for excellent service. The diploma allowed her to teach anywhere in the state, but she chose to stay right where she was.

Miss Griffith was again called to public service in 1910. State Superintendent of Public Instruction Helen M. Wixson appointed her deputy superintendent of that department. The appointment boosted Emily's prestige and knowledge of how educational needs were addressed at the official level. The job often took her into schools and classrooms around the state, broadening her viewpoint. "She began," as biographer Elinor Bluemel put it, "to realize the power of her personality."

Her two years in the public instruction post were well spent, but in 1913, School Superintendent Dr. Charles E. Chadsey insisted she return to Twenty-fourth Street School, largely because of her proven disciplinary ability. Emily gladly complied. Moreover, she committed herself from that time forward to serving the disadvantaged of the community by reshaping public education.

The night classes she taught in the old Longfellow School were described in a January 24, 1914, feature story in the *Rocky Mountain News*. "All Nations Study at Night School to Be Americans," read the headline. "There were men and women, boys and girls; they came from the East, West, North and South. Jews from Russia, men from Bulgaria, Germany, and Greece, several Swedish girls. Austrians, Finlanders, Chinese and Japanese. From every corner of the world they came—and all to learn English—to become American citizens.

"The foreign rooms are only one feature of the night school," the story continued, further describing a sewing room where working girls and women came to make their own clothes. One young girl was busy over baby clothes, while another was creating her entire trousseau. "And in the cooking room, how busy and happy! Many a prospective bride [was] learning to make coffee and bread 'just the kind that mother makes, too.'"

With the coming of telephones, moving pictures, trolleys and motorcars, daily life was changing. An optimistic spirit of reform infused Denver as it did the rest of the country. In the midst of the Progressive Era, the time had come for the realization of her dream. Leveraging the prodigious combination of her new political connections and her natural teaching ability, Emily Griffith began her long personal crusade for the educationally disenfranchised of the Mile High City.

3
With the Flow

Even amid the show homes of Denver's Capitol Hill neighborhood, the relatively new mansion at 400 East 8th Avenue was a standout. Emily Griffith felt like a fish out of water as she entered the commanding front hallway. The broad, columned corridor featured ornate French chandeliers, and 100 feet beyond the foyer, a broad bay window framed a view of distant Pikes Peak.

The butler who took her wrap mentioned in respectful tones that his nephew had been in Miss Griffith's sixth-grade class at Central School several years earlier. When she heard his name, Emily remembered the boy, as she did nearly every student who passed through her tutelage. Before she could inquire into the young man's current circumstances, the hostess approached to greet her.

The gracious and beautiful Mrs. Walter Cheesman turned to put an arm about the waist of a younger woman who joined them and introduced her as her daughter, Gladys Cheesman Evans. Emily smiled and politely shook the hands of both women, complimenting their home which, Mrs. Cheesman noted proudly, Gladys had helped her father to design, along with architects Movean and Norton.

The result of their efforts was a graceful, soaring home of three stories. The semicircular west portico featured a two-story Ionic colonnade. Elegant architectural elements such as high arched windows and a widow's walk made the mansion the envy of local high society. Emily was escorted to the spacious, marble-floored Palm Room, a circular solarium filled with Italian statuary and large potted plants. She gazed out tall windows at the far end, overlooking an illuminated fountain and lily pond in the rose garden.[1]

She was impressed, but not intimidated, by the opulence that surrounded her. The gilded mirrors and the sumptuous furnishings bespoke an affluence worlds removed from the Five Points setting of her Twenty-fourth Street School. That was precisely why she was here. These were women of wealth and, consequently, of influence—women who, if sufficiently inspired, could affect dramatic reform in a significant way. Emily was determined, as the evening's speaker, to persuade them to support the cause most dear to her heart.

Following the ladies' club's brief business meeting, Emily was introduced as a former deputy state superintendent of schools and of public instruction. The titles elicited respect and hushed anticipation from the members assembled as she stepped to the podium.

In her soft but clear teacher's voice, she told them about her long-cherished dream. This opening caught the attention of any group she addressed. She had spoken to many in recent years. Never did she lecture, preach, cajole, or push. Emily's instructive style was to take her listeners to a comfortable overlook and bid them to gaze beyond.

When she spoke to ladies' clubs, emphasis on civic improvement struck a chord with her audience. The sweet-voiced Miss Griffith spoke with earnest enthusiasm about how public education for adults could create better citizens and, by extension, enhance civic pride. Give folks the skills to support themselves and their families adequately, she reasoned, and poverty and the social ills that so often accompany it will lose their grip on the city.

The purpose of education, to Emily's mind, should be to prepare people for a useful role in society. Public school must work to "fit folks to life."[2] Denver Public Schools, she proposed, should offer whatever that mission might entail—be it basic reading and figuring skills, English for the foreign born, or skills that could lead directly to a better job or a promotion.

She may have referenced Denver Mayor Robert Speer's recent but controversial "City Beautiful" civic improvements. Do impressive monuments and expanded parks make a city great, when ugly social circumstances continue to darken the daily lives of so many of its residents? Emily and other reformers asked. A way must be found to lift people out of the bewildering and demoralizing situations in which she found them every day, Emily concluded fervently, persuading her audience of public education's responsibility to provide a helping hand to folks of all ages and backgrounds.

The assembled socialites nodded in agreement and murmured affirmative comments behind gloved hands. What the reformist teacher proposed seemed both sensible and simple. They applauded politely at the end of her talk. As usually happened, some dismissed her idealistic ideas as soon as tea and refreshments were served.

A few ladies, however, were genuinely affected and drew Miss Griffith aside before leaving. The school she envisioned had the potential to uplift Denver's disadvantaged and improve the general citizenry of their fair city. Like others, they wanted to help.

———

Long before the strategy had a name, Emily Griffith recognized the power of networking. Every successful campaign benefits from strategic allies, and the drive to make the opportunity school a reality was no exception. Her years as both a teacher and a public administrator had drawn Emily into many and diverse circles, and from each she drew substantial support for her cause.

The proliferation of ladies' clubs was an American phenomenon of the late nineteenth and early twentieth centuries. The Victorian Age had charged women with the moral guardianship of the family. Now women were expanding their scope of responsibility, gradually moving from homemaking to tidying up their broader communities. Women's movements for temperance, suffrage, and the abolition of vices such as prostitution aimed to reform society as a whole. Women began to realize the power of their confederation. They campaigned for—and won—public libraries, free kindergartens, and schools for the handicapped and the delinquent. They insisted upon medical examinations for schoolchildren and more humane conditions for working women and children.

The women's club movement in Colorado exceeded national trends. In this boom-and-bust, male-dominated part of the country, the fairer sex were especially hungry for social interaction and intellectual stimulation. Colorado even formed its own Federation of Women's Clubs in 1895, following the national model established five years earlier to encompass no less than 500 organizations across the country with more than 100,000 total members. Groups with names such as the Clio Club (after the Greek muse of history) met to hold discussions of literature and drama. In his 1901 *History of Denver*, Jerome Smiley quoted a local pundit who declared "for a city of its size, Denver is club mad."

Colorado women's club members, led by Virginia McClurg and Lucy Peabody, championed the movement to protect and preserve the ancient cliff dwellings of Mesa Verde by securing national park designation for the site in 1906. Pressure from women's clubs played no small role in the 1912 law outlawing prostitution in Denver and impelled the 1916 statewide prohibition on alcoholic beverages, four years before the nation went dry. Women were beginning to flex their collective muscles and shift their focus from study to action through these clubs. In them, social reformers such as Emily found ardent subscribers.

Emily partnered with other community factions as well. Her relationship with social workers developed naturally from her first days of teaching and home visits in Denver. To social workers, she advocated adult education as an effective countermeasure to the destitution and despair that manifested itself in unemployment, domestic violence, substance abuse, and crime. She built alliances with the Social Services Bureau, City Charities, the Red Cross, the Jewish Aid Society, the Federal Naturalization Bureau, the YMCA and YWCA, the Child Placement Department of Public Schools, the Juvenile Court, the Mothers' Compensation Group, Big Brothers, churches, jails, and numerous other organizations that dealt with social problems.

Businessmen's organizations, too, were gradually receptive to the attractive little lady's proposal. By virtue of her membership in the Central Presbyterian Church, she was acquainted with some of the most successful bankers and businessmen in Denver. In addressing their clubs and associations, Emily decried the waste of potential workers who lacked basic or specific skills requisite for gainful employment. She presented the economic logic of mobilizing these human resources. When she spoke of her school as an investment, and of its graduates as a valuable product, business leaders listened.

The concepts of adult education, night school, vocational education, and English as a second language did not originate with Emily Griffith. Programs in all of these areas already existed in Denver and many other places throughout the country. A movement for technical and trade schools had been gathering steam since the 1890s. Denver's Manual Training High School was founded on "the idea that the mind might be trained through the hands…as well as through books."[3] Two of the six class periods each day were devoted to trade skills: forge and machine shop for boys; cooking, sewing, and millinery for girls. Woodworking and mechanical drawing were required of everyone for graduation from the three-year program.

Denver's Modern School of Business ran advertisements offering adult classes in shorthand and bookkeeping, and the School of Advanced Stenography touted "speed" courses in ads interspersed throughout newspaper "Help Wanted" pages. Schools as far away as California sought to lure future electricians or welders. But private training did not come cheap.

The 1915 Denver Public Schools' survey of existing adult literacy classes listed evening classes in two buildings—Longfellow Elementary and Manual High—serving 1,222 students. A few local churches offered classes in English and American government for immigrants seeking naturalization. Vocational training was also provided by Moler Barber College, Mountain States Telephone and Telegraph, Denver Gas and Electric, and the YMCA.

What was new and visionary about Griffith's proposed school was that it would bring adult basic education, immigrant education, and vocational education under the public schools umbrella. It would be free and open to all Denver residents. It would offer classes both day and night, for young and old together. It would be free of the existing limitations of fees, restricted hours, amateur instruction, and admissions and graduation requirements. Her school would be the first in the world to offer this unique arrangement of educational opportunities.[4]

Timing was key to Emily's success. The mood of the country in the early twentieth century was in her favor. People believed above all in progress—the continual, albeit often uneven, upward surge of civilization. Improvements to the physical and social environment were thought to lead inevitably to improvements in humankind itself.

President Teddy Roosevelt embodied the affirmation, confidence, and optimism found throughout the land. America believed itself to be the Land of Opportunity, where even the poorest immigrant or lowliest laborer could improve his or her lot. Equalizing the chances of success for the underprivileged ought, by extension, to be a responsibility of government at every level. Miss Griffith's concept of a public opportunity school spoke directly to this emerging national conscience.

Civic groups, chambers of commerce, and social reformers were charmed by the gently crusading schoolteacher and convinced of the merits of the universal public instruction she championed. Educators, on the other hand, were quite another matter.

The stiffest opposition to her idea came from those in Emily's own profession. Critics throughout the Denver public school system found her proposal for a school without admissions or even attendance requirements bordering on the blasphemous. The standards of education would be lowered to unacceptable levels, they protested. Students can't simply drop in whenever they like to learn whatever they want. Outrageous! Unprecedented! What teacher could possibly be expected to cope with such chaos? Rules, restrictions, prescribed curricula, and measurable results were considered the very foundations of organized education.

All too frequently, attacks were leveled at Emily personally. Traditional educators pointed out that Miss Griffith's own formal education had ended with the eighth grade. How could any legitimate academic take seriously the bold scheme of someone who had not even earned a high school diploma, let alone attempted a single college course? Was it any wonder she seemed unable to grasp how inappropriate and unfeasible this school she envisioned would be? Only one unversed in higher education, they argued, could so woefully misinterpret the role and the mission of public instruction.

These personal assaults by her colleagues must have affected Emily deeply. But they did not daunt her. Never known for her impressive vocabulary or oratory technique, she knew instead how to tell personal stories and how to express heartfelt concern for the educationally underserved. With this simple, genuine approach, she won over both individuals and audiences. She was making inroads, to be sure. By the winter of 1915, Emily Griffith was poised to enlist one of her most influential allies.

4
Spring Thaw

On a chilly but sunny afternoon in early December 1915, reporter Frances Wayne glanced up from the morning edition and gazed out the third-story window of her Champa Street *Denver Post* office. Ideal weather had animated the holiday shoppers crowding the downtown streets below.

"Half Million Dollars is Spent in Single Day, Says Merchant" proclaimed the headline over a photomontage. "Christmas Shoppers Pack Streets and Swoop Down Upon Every Store." Advertisements in the *Post*'s pages had surely helped to fuel the frenzy. Victrolas and pianolas were the high-tech innovations of the day, and everybody wanted to one-up the neighbors by being the first to own one. For only $24, a Victor Talking Machine could reproduce "His Master's Voice" in your very own parlor. The Denver Music Company touted Baldwin's "Manualoo—the player piano that is all but human," from $550 (easy payment plans available, of course).

Daniels & Fisher's Bargain Basement offered women's gloves for $1.50 a pair and ladies' coats for $9.75. Joslin's Dry Goods, "The Store with the Christmas Spirit," advertised "A splendid opportunity to buy Christmas furs: Many odd pieces—mink, muskrat, skunk, and moleskin—muffs, scarves, and neckpieces, $10–$15."

An ad for the Lewis Store proclaimed, "Only Three Weeks to Practice the Great Glad Game," a gimmick taken from the popular novel, *Pollyanna*, about an optimistic young girl determined to find something in everything to be glad about. The advertisement outlined the "rules" of the game thusly: "Fees to Pay for Cost of Organization—

Smiles. Certificate—A neat little button-pin to be worn on all occasions, bearing the inscription 'I'm playing the GLAD GAME; are you?'"

As organizer of the *Post*'s Big Brothers Christmas charity drive for the past several years, Frances Wayne could not help but contrast the privileged middle-class children, who were dreaming of Lewis's Toyland and "the most wonderful assortment ever" of dolls and mechanical trains, with the impoverished youngsters in endless lines that stretched daily outside the *Post*'s offices. She headed downstairs to face the needy throngs again.

"Share Your Christmas with Poor Youngsters and Join Big Brothers," Wayne pleaded in her regular columns. "Hundreds of Ragged Little Urchins Waiting for Warm Clothes and Shoes…Small Gift on Your Part Means Real Happiness to Them."

Every donation, no matter how large or small, was acknowledged in the *Post*, though many generous folks wished to be known only as "Big Sister," "A Friend," or "A Mother of Three." By and large, both individuals and businesses seemed inclined toward greater generosity as 1915 drew to a close. At the same time, the needs of Denver's poor were overwhelming. For desperate children awaiting shoes and coats before the weather deteriorated, the Great Glad Game was an everyday challenge.

Wayne sighed as she opened the door to the downstairs donations room. A tiny, tidy auburn-haired woman smiled warmly as she brushed past, shepherding more than a dozen shabby but hopeful youngsters toward tables heaped high with donated clothing and footwear. A boy sorting through mounds of mittens called for his teacher to help find a match. A girl trying on a secondhand coat spun around for approval. Another needed help buckling an overshoe, while yet another cried that he'd lost his own shoe in the pile. It seemed to Wayne that everyone was clamoring for "Miss Griffith" at once, yet the indefatigable teacher smiled and laughed and never lost patience. Pollyanna herself would be hard-pressed to match this dynamo of positivism.

Ace reporter Frances Wayne was impressed. She knew the genuine article when she saw it. This diminutive schoolmarm determined to outfit her devoted charges was something special. When at last every one of her pupils had been fitted with winter wear, Griffith stayed behind to help rearrange the scattered mounds of scarves, gloves, and hats. Many years later, Wayne recounted her memory of this first meeting, and the words Emily Griffith used to describe her earnest proposal:

> I wonder if you will let me tell you of a hope I have for the people in and out of my school—the boys and girls, their parents, too, whose education has been limited by poverty?
>
> I want to help to establish a school where the clock will be stopped from morning until midnight. I want the age limit for admission to be lifted and the classes so arranged that a boy or girl working in a bakery, store, laundry or any kind of shop who has an hour or two to spare may come to school, study what he or she wants to learn to make life more useful.
>
> The same rule goes for older folks, too. I know I will be laughed at, but what of it?...I already have a name for that school. It is Opportunity.[1]

———

Long before the fictional Lois Lane and Brenda Starr inspired young women to pursue newspaper careers, Frances "Pinky" Wayne was a real-life intrepid female reporter. Editors tried to relegate her to the traditional female corners of journalism—society news, arts criticism, and tear-jerking features. It wasn't long, however, before the irrepressible redhead was covering fires, murder trials, and politics with the "big boys" and championing one social reform after another.

Frances Belford, named for her mother, was born in Indiana in 1870, and soon thereafter moved with her family to Central City during its mining heyday. When her father, James B. Belford, a territorial supreme court judge, was elected the first Colorado representative to the U.S. House, the family relocated to Washington, D.C., where Frances spent most of her formative years. It's no surprise that her interest in politics and public affairs began early.

"Pinky" (so dubbed by a classmate for her hair color) had a personality as fiery as her tresses. Her early marriage to John Anthony Wayne seems to have lasted only long enough to effect her surname change.

Although her Denver newspaper career began in 1906 at the *Rocky Mountain News,* she was soon lured away by the *Denver Post* when the *Post*'s art critic passed away. Her flowery journalistic style and occasional moralizing were in keeping with the times.

What Wayne called the greatest friendship of her life began the day Emily Griffith escorted her Twenty-fourth Street School pupils to the *Denver Post*'s offices. When Emily stayed behind to help rearrange the heaps of donated garments her needy students had disheveled in their excitement, the reporter and the teacher began to get acquainted.

Emily had confessed that she had turned down an invitation to a house party to escort the children, but her tone registered not the slightest regret. She confided, without a trace of cynicism, her hidden agenda: Were she not there to supervise, the youngsters might take articles not suited to themselves at all—to sell. She couldn't blame them. How else were they to buy Christmas gifts for their family members?

Their conversation revolved around the plight of the city's poor. Thanks to the relentless crusading of the Women's Christian Temperance Union, Colorado was poised to "go dry" on New Year's Day 1916, less than a month away. The imminent ban on the sale of alcohol would mitigate some social problems, but it would surely exacerbate others by eliminating jobs in breweries, liquor distribution, liquor stores, bars, and saloons throughout the state. Those workers unemployed who did not choose to leave the state would have to adapt by finding other lines of work. But how could they—or any of the unemployed—succeed in a new occupation without practical training?

Most of the impoverished children of Denver came from households headed by unemployed fathers or single mothers who were unable to support their families. The schoolteacher and the reporter were of like minds and united in their goal. They agreed that the problem was too pervasive to be assuaged by a Christmas charity drive, however generous. Emily insisted that something else was needed. More than a handout, these people needed a hand up.

Wayne could see that behind Emily Griffith's soft blue eyes smoldered the spark of a determined reformer. The little woman who had taught and worked with disadvantaged populations since the age of sixteen described her long-held dream to her new acquaintance, who soon became one of her closest friends and staunchest advocates.

In the weeks and months ahead, Emily Griffith elaborated on her big idea to Frances Wayne. What she envisioned was a school that met the immediate needs of people and of employers. It would be a school that offered public instruction in basic academics for those who had somehow missed out, as well as English for the foreign-born, and specialized job skills. Emily's personal teaching mission was focused on those outside the mainstream of public education—the misfits, the dropouts, immigrants and minorities, the unemployed and the underemployed. Hers would be a second chance school for those with a sincere desire to improve their lot in life through practical education.

Wayne soon realized that what Griffith's mission represented was much more than a remedial tonic for social ills. It was, in fact, the prescription for an effective long-term treatment and, conceivably, a cure.

No one could manipulate public opinion in Denver like the *Post*'s Frances Wayne. Over the years, she persuaded her loyal readers to support such causes as community Christmas lighting, one of the nation's first juvenile court systems, and the sweeping public health reforms of Dr. Florence Sabin. Perhaps more than any of her other campaigns, Wayne took a personal interest in Griffith's Opportunity School proposal.

According to author Elinor Bluemel in her 1954 biography of Griffith, Wayne was so enthusiastic about the Opportunity School idea that she "offered to give it a hearing in the Press." Bluemel creates the impression that subsequent publicity in the *Post* was directly responsible for rallying community support for the cause and persuading school board members. The reality, however, is that no mention of Miss Griffith or her Opportunity School concept—by Frances Wayne or any other writer—appeared in the *Denver Post* until two days after the proposal received official approval.[2]

The fact that Bluemel got this part of the story from Emily Griffith herself may go a long way toward explaining the discrepancy. Emily was often quoted as saying, "Without the support of Frances Wayne, the Opportunity School would have remained just a dream."[3] Griffith was an unassuming person, more comfortable attributing success to others than taking credit for her own hard work, effective networking, and personal persuasiveness.

Nonetheless, if Emily was an evangelist for practical education, Wayne was surely her most influential disciple. The reporter undoubtedly did substantial campaigning behind the scenes, if not in print, to get community movers and shakers, such as her *Post* editors, Fred Bonfils and Harry Tammen, onboard the Opportunity School bandwagon.

By spring of the following year, the Denver school board was being pressured by businessmen, welfare groups, civic organizations, influential individuals, and public opinion in general to give Emily's proposal a chance. Wayne recalled, "The day she was to present her new idea to the Denver Board of Education, she admitted, 'I'm trembling like a leaf because perhaps I am too ambitious. For myself, I really want nothing.'"[4]

The school board met briefly on Thursday, May 11, 1916, to handled important business that had been delayed since February. Superintendent Carlos Cole recommended that the old Longfellow School building be repaired and equipped as an "opportunity school," opened both day and night, with Miss Emily Griffith appointed principal at $1,800 per year for her services. It was moved by Stephen Knight and seconded by Chester Morey that the recommendation be adopted. The favorable vote was unanimous. At long last, the revolutionary idea germinated years earlier on the Nebraska prairie had a chance to take root—right in the heart of downtown Denver.

5

From Trickle to Stream

An immigrant arriving at Union Station on one of the many railroad lines serving Denver in 1916 could find a printed card in his native language, describing a school where he might come to learn English and "Americanization" for free. A tired laundress, heading home after a day of washing for those better off, might see on the side of her streetcar an advertisement for the new public school where anyone—even she—might learn the skills of a less physically draining trade, such as typing or millinery.

Without the benefit of any formal training in sales theory or technique, Emily Griffith was a marketing natural who knew how to reach her targeted audience. Where they arrived, where they settled, where they toiled, she spread the word of Opportunity. It was a potent, evocative word that meant, in any language, a chance and a hope for something better.

As soon as her idea got the school board's seal of approval, Emily wasted no time shifting from persuader to promoter. The pitch she'd been delivering to potential supporters for years now became her recruitment call to potential students.

Denver Post reporter Marie La Due interviewed Emily the day after the school board's green light. The *Post* provided Emily's first public platform to talk about the new school. The caption beneath the pleasant photo of Miss Griffith, "progressive Denver school teacher, popularly known as 'The Little Mother of the Twenty-fourth Street School,'" promised a place where anyone, regardless of age, race, or gender, "may drop in any hour of the day or night and get practical training in what-ever line interests them."[1]

"Everything One Wants to Know About Earning a Living Taught," one subheading promised, as well as "How to Find and Hold Jobs." The staff of any college career center, vocational school placement office, or employment agency will confirm that the appeal of such practical training is as strong today as it was in the years immediately preceding America's entry into the First World War. Learning for its own sake is all well and good, but the application of knowledge to gainful employment is where the real payoff lies.

Cooperation with local businessmen was key to the school's mis-sion, Griffith emphasized in the story. The curriculum incorporated employers' suggestions about the preparation their staff and appren-tices needed. "The school will have for its foundation a vocational guidance bureau which will study Denver's needs and guide boys and girls into work where there is a future for them. We will also have a follow up system for [those students] who go to work—Why doesn't he make good? Why does he lose his job? We will find out and remedy these things." To many readers, Miss Griffith's new school must have sounded too good to be true.

"We will help the foreign man to become a real citizen, not just a naturalized one. We will teach the foreign woman the English language and American ways, so the tragedy of the scorn of her English-speaking children will not cut into her life.

"When the older children are in school, she can take the babies and go to the Opportunity School. There her [young] children will be cared for while she learns to save money by making their clothes,...to cook nourishing food for them, to care properly for their bodies, and to buy properly for the family, instead of being robbed by the merchant with shabby materials and unreasonable prices."

An illustrative drawing alongside Griffith's photo accompanied the *Post* story. People were depicted ascending stairs labeled "Opportunity" and "Industry," and the beneficent lady on the uppermost step, surrounded by dawning rays of light, reached down to take both hands of one aspiring toward the top. This simple representation of the school's mission effectively conveyed Opportunity School's hopeful message to all who longed to uplift themselves.

From 8:30 a.m. until 10:00 p.m., the school would offer people of all ages and backgrounds a self-prescribed education in manageable doses as their individual situations demanded or allowed. Now older folks might nibble at the basic skills routinely force-fed youngsters by public schools, or learn "the technical things which will make them the world's workers instead of the world's drudges."[2]

Longfellow School, the thirty-four-year-old building designated for this pilot program, had been condemned before the eleventh-hour reprieve. Abandoned except for a few night classes, the neglected building required some serious repairs and sprucing up before it was fit to welcome students in September. The school board authorized replacement of the windows with larger ones of blue and red stained glass to improve lighting and ventilation. They funded minor repairs and painting, but when no funds for cleanup were forthcoming, Emily and her staff scrubbed and mopped every inch of the place themselves.

Several of Griffith's former students, who were enrolled in Manual Training High School, created a sign to mount above the new school's entrance. In gold-leaf paint, the shining letters proudly proclaimed "Public Opportunity School—For All Who Wish to Learn," the very words Emily remembered from the sign on her uncle's canal boat all those years ago in Ohio.

The acquisition of equipment and supplies presented its own difficulties. The school board was reluctant to allocate much to the unprecedented project without hard facts. How many students were expected? What were they going to study? How many classrooms were needed? How many desks?

Miss Griffith simply could not say. She could tell them only that there would be no admissions requirements and that no one would be turned away. She could tell them that students would be asked what they wished to learn, not told what they must. She could tell them that there would be no attendance mandates, and that students could drop into and out of classes whenever they chose. They might come for just a few hours a day; they might stay for just a few days or a few weeks. Some of the classes would require student desks, but others would need shop setups or other nontraditional arrangements.

The school board allotted desks for two classrooms, the teachers and the principal; a typewriter; a portable blackboard; and a box of chalk. Thus equipped, the staff of Opportunity faced its first day of operation on September 9, 1916.

Emily Griffith arrived at the school very early that morning, dressed in one of the white frilly frocks she favored, anxious in every sense of the word. She was excited to see her long-held vision materialize. But what exactly was it going to look like? What if no one came? Or worse, what if they came only to scoff or criticize?

If her confidence or conviction wavered briefly, she banished any doubts upon the arrival of the five teachers she had personally selected. To them, she showed only determined optimism and enthusiasm as they prepared to welcome all who sought their help. Miss Griffith set up her principal's desk in the hallway, right inside the entrance to warmly greet each person as they entered. The doors were opened, and Denver's Public Opportunity School welcomed its first pupils.

Emily's effective marketing bore fruit that very first morning. Streetcar after streetcar stopped at the intersection of 13th and Welton, delivering the hopeful and the hesitant, the curious and the desperate—each with his or her own reasons for seeking admittance to this school like no other.

"Don't bother with enrollment cards," Emily advised Assistant Principal Mary Fenton Miller and the rest of her staff. "Too many questions might put people off. Find out first what they want."[3] They wanted all sorts of things: blueprint reading, hat decorating, English instruction, bicycle repair, masonry, sewing, housemaid training. Adults wanted to finish the eighth grade, young people wanted to qualify for apprenticeships, immigrants wanted preparation for the citizenship examination.

Emily had optimistically hoped for as many as 200 students. By the end of the first week, more than 1,400 people had enrolled in Opportunity School. The challenges of meeting an enrollment six times greater than expected were enormous. No staff of five, however talented and resourceful, could begin to manage such numbers and such varied requests. Part-time instructors were recruited from local businesses and industries, as well as the Denver public school system. Emily's youngest sister, Ethelyn, was among her first hires.

Space was at a premium from the start. More than one class had to meet on the back steps. Equipment and supplies were woefully inadequate. More than a hundred people signed up to learn typing on the school's one typewriter in the first week. Creative solutions could accomplish only so much. Armed at last with real—and impressive—numbers, Griffith found the school board much more responsive to her requests.

As a general guideline, Opportunity created a class if twenty people expressed a desire for it. One of the first offered was housemaid training. The shortage of domestic help in Denver was acute, in no small part because women employed in the homemaking arts resented being considered servants. Balancing these objections with a crucial need in the community, Emily struck upon a politically correct title for those who completed Opportunity's course. They were designated "housekeeper assistants." She often employed graduates of this program when she held dinner parties and proudly credited them in front of her guests with planning and executing every detail of the evening.

The automobile course instituted that January was the first ever offered by a public educational institution. The 146 day and evening students who signed up for the course were taught much more than engine repair. R. L. Green, a gas engine specialist and former instructor at the State Teachers College in Greeley, headed the program and lectured each class for 45 minutes a day on the theoretical principals governing mechanics, rudiments of physics, and the construction and operation of automobiles. His two assistants then took over for hands-on instruction in the shop, where students had the opportunity to dissemble and reassemble automobile parts and systems. The course prepared students for employment in garages, repair shops, or automobile manufacturing plants. Employers, who could not afford to teach their employees and pay them at the same time, were staunch supporters of the program.

Pupils in the automobile course were as young as sixteen. Not all planned on making the work a career, and not all were male. Many car owners or prospective owners enrolled to learn how to take care of their new machines. The training cost none of them a thing but time and effort, and anyone was eligible.

Barbering had been taught in vocational schools for many years, but Opportunity was one of the first schools in the nation to offer a training program for those who wished to work in beauty parlors. With the popularity of bobbed hair, hairstyling was an up-and-coming profession, and Emily recognized the potential. The offer of cheap haircuts and beauty treatments by students attracted the public.

Each morning, Miss Griffith wrote a message on the chalkboard beside her front hall desk. One of her favorites was "You Can Do It"— an encouraging reassurance to her staff and students alike. Emily chose teachers much like herself, teachers with experience in one-room schoolhouses or other circumstances requiring mastery of individualized instruction for students of all ages and abilities within the same class. Opportunity School teachers had to be flexible, versatile, adaptable, and ingenious.

The school was open thirteen hours a day, five days a week. Students arrived and departed at any time. Another of her chalkboard messages read, "Come when you can. Enter your classes whenever you get here. We know you try to be on time." Rigid, schedule-bound instruction went out the window. It was not the place, Griffith once observed, for nervous teachers.[4]

It was, instead, known from the first day as "the friendly school." Principal Griffith insisted upon that. She recognized that many who came to Opportunity bore the emotional baggage of unfortunate previous school experiences or uncaring teachers. Others were inhibited by the stigma that seeking education meant first admitting their ignorance. Emily liked to say, "We took people just as they came."[5] Opportunity teachers were sensitive to each individual's emotional as well as academic needs. Instilling confidence and self-esteem was every bit as important to them as imparting useful skills.

Everyone who came to the school sought vocational preparation in one form or another. Whether they needed enough basic math to be a carpenter, adequate English skills to conduct business in their new country, or advanced training to win a promotion, Griffith found a way to provide it. She drew upon her vast network of connections within the greater community as a resource for vocational course content. Classes in electricity, for example, were planned by and associated with the Denver Gas and Electric Company, training workers in exactly the way the employer wanted. Colorado State Agricultural College (now Colorado State University) cooperated with Opportunity, teaching city boys the basics of agriculture to prepare them for summer jobs on farms and ranches across the state. Short courses in dressmaking and millinery were taught by adjunct professionals in those fields.

Millinery, or hat design, was one of the most popular courses in the school's early curriculum. Emily is often pictured wearing extravagant and unique chapeaux created by students. Prostitution had been outlawed in Denver a few years before, leaving a number of young women in need of vocational training. The pursuit of a new, fashionable career may very well have drawn more than one such "soiled dove" to Opportunity.

Griffith emphasized that the school was not for "down-and-outers." It was, instead, the place to find a second chance—or a third or a tenth. Earnest tries were not limited, and past failures were overlooked. Desire to learn and effort applied were what counted. Opportunity welcomed those who had no other place to turn to for the training or education they needed. Former criminals, the mentally or physically impaired, and others excluded from mainstream education were welcomed at Miss Griffith's school. "They are the ones we can help most," the compassionate principal insisted.[6]

Immigrants, too, found a home and a helping hand at Opportunity. In addition to classes akin to what is now called English as a Second Language (ESL), courses in "Americanization" helped the foreign-born student navigate the often bewildering U.S. culture. Germans, Irish, Poles, French, Scandinavians, Greeks, Russians, British, Italians, Chinese, and Hispanics found their way to Denver in search of freedoms and a new life. The local U.S. Naturalization Service sent new arrivals from all nations straight to Opportunity to learn what they needed to know to become citizens. Emily sought to mitigate the neglect and prejudice so often faced by immigrants. She recognized how important it was that new Americans be educated in their rights and responsibilities.

She also understood, from her "boarding around" days as a young prairie schoolmarm, how much it meant to connect with others from one's homeland. When a Swedish student, for example, first arrived at Opportunity, Emily personally saw to it that the newcomer was introduced to, and taken under the wing of, Swedish veterans of the English and citizenship programs. Every foreign-born student carried a card that read: "The bearer of this card is a student at the Opportunity School and is worthy of your respect."[7]

Early in the school's fledgling period, a young man in one of Emily's evening classes fainted in mid-recitation. She learned that he had come directly to school after working a 10-hour shift and had not eaten all day. Correctly deducing that this was not an isolated case, Griffith implemented what may have been the progenitor of free lunch programs in public schools. Every day for nearly two years, Emily and her sister Florence brought big pails of soup made by their mother from 1524 Fillmore Street to the school on the Colfax streetcar. They served more than 200 bowls nightly in the basement kitchen. Emily's hall chalkboard message, "A bowl of soup is served from 5:30 to 7:30 FREE. This saves you time,"[8] made it sound like a simple matter of efficiency rather than charity.

The daily soup-bucket brigade was finally retired when a wealthy woman anonymously arranged to have soup ingredients delivered to the school daily so that it could be made on the premises. The light meal available at no charge was a godsend to those who went straight from work to classes, either because of time restrictions or because they could not afford the double carfare to go home, then to school, and back home again. Principal Griffith also kept a pocket full of nickels for the streetcar riders among her pupils.

Emily was particularly interested in attracting boys and girls who were about to finish the eighth grade and had no plans to go on to high school. Instead of drifting into trouble or low-paying jobs, they were actively recruited by Opportunity School, where they could learn not only vocation-specific skills, but general employment skills as well.

"WANTED: All Boys and Girls to come to the Opportunity School," began the classified advertisement run in local newspapers. "Talk it over with Miss Griffith and find out why you didn't hold that job. Learn how to get and hold a better one."[9]

Students were coached on how to present themselves to employers and how to dress professionally. The school provided those who could not afford such things with respectable suits, dresses, and shoes donated by generous civic organizations. How to complete an employment application, how to prepare for a job interview, and basic employment behaviors, such as reporting for work consistently and on time, were all part of Opportunity's employment success package.

Opportunity School had not yet celebrated its first anniversary when the United States entered World War I. President Woodrow Wilson signed the Smith-Hughes Act, authorizing $7.2 million for public vocational education. Emily Griffith accepted federal funds with reservations; she feared government intervention in education and believed that Opportunity should not depend upon government financial support any more than individuals should.

Principal Griffith and her staff earned the government money. They were soon training Denver's citizens in radio communications, gas engine maintenance and repair, ambulance driving, drafting, nursing, and first aid—all useful skills in the war effort.

The May 18, 1917, *Denver Post* ran a photo feature story headlined "Six Girls Put on Overalls and Take Jobs in Shops." "Gee, I've always wanted a boy's job, and now I've got a chance to use my muscles," declared Marie Thomas, one of the first girls trained at the Opportunity School as a lathe operator to take the place of enlisted men at the Denver Rock Drill Manufacturing Company. The employer was so pleased that sixty young women were hired—at the same wage as the men they replaced—to work in the machine shops. "The company has fitted up lunch and rest rooms for its women employees," the *Post* reported, "and on their part the girls have guaranteed to stick to the machinist's trade."

During the war, aviation mechanics were taught using a plane donated to the school. Classes filled to capacity, and students wound up on waiting lists. By April 1918, 125 men from Opportunity were working as wireless operators. The school's service flag boasted 247 stars—one for each student serving in the armed forces. The stars represented twenty different nationalities.

For their part, female pupils devoted one afternoon a week to recycling old, worn-out items into baby clothes for the Allies. More than 8,000 garments were sent to France, Belgium, and Italy from Opportunity.

"The school is democratic," declared one newspaper story. "It provides training for the energetic person anxious to get ahead; the discouraged one trying to get into line again; the man who missed his schooling; the educated taking some special training; the working boy and girl who come at odd times, and in fact all shades and degrees of both rich and poor. Often servant and mistress make hats at the same table."[10]

By the end of the 1916–1917 academic year, the new Opportunity School had served 2,378 pupils with 38 staff. Exact counts were difficult to nail down, as students dropped in and dropped out, and attendance was not obsessively tracked. Average daytime attendance was conservatively estimated at 200, while evening classes accommodated twice that number at any given time.

The next two years at Opportunity saw the addition of classes in waitressing and shorthand, wallpaper hanging and bricklaying, and complete business courses. Curriculum responded to student demand and employer needs. Miss Griffith got employers to slip notices into pay envelopes telling workers that new classes would be started upon request.

Speed stenography proved extremely popular. During the war, "stenographers had been boosted to the class of pigeon-blood rubies because they were so rare," claimed *Post* reporter Frances Wayne. "Now, through the designs of Emily Griffith, every stenographer with brains in her or his head and a desire to use them may win the title of 'competent'." Students provided a notebook and pencil, and Opportunity provided instruction in taking dictation for the civil service, railroad, law, or general offices. They learned how to fill out insurance and legal forms, as well, preparing them to "make a fine living through competent service."[11]

Western Union arranged for hundreds of messenger boys to spend an hour a day at the school. Their bicycles crowded its sidewalks and basement hallways. Boys who worked in a large confectionary kitchen and lunchroom downtown also went to school for several hours a day on the employer's time, learning to become better, more skilled employees. Tramway workers did as well.

Soon the school had established its own store to teach all aspects of the retail trade, as well as a bank run not only for instructional purposes, but also as a service to other students and their families.

Results were impressive. A machinist who learned drafting doubled his salary. A man who had measured out muslin for ten years found happiness as a bookkeeper. A drifting boy found his calling in a railroad telegraphy class and quit the pool halls for employment. A woman with hands grown rough from years of laundry work excelled at stitching dainty Sunday hats. The success stories were as numerous as Opportunity's alumni.

The secret of the Opportunity School's early success was no secret at all. It was Emily Griffith's generous, pragmatic, and democratic vision. She determined to offer folks whatever it was they had missed out on in life, whatever it was they needed to be self-sufficient, productive, and hopeful.

"Who is Denver's most useful citizen?" Frances Wayne asked in her September 1919 *Denver Post* story, "If the question were put to a vote... it is likely that Miss Emily Griffith, founder and principal of Opportunity School, would be named by an overwhelming majority."

"There is at least one thing in life that a person can do well," Principal Griffith challenged her colleagues. "Let's find out what it is."[12] Society's misfits, she believed, were those who had selected, or had had selected for them, the wrong occupation, one for which they were simply not suited. One illustrative example was an energetic and self-reliant homeschooled girl who came to Opportunity from a small town in the mountains with the intention of learning stenography. She managed the work all right, but it held no challenge or gratification for her. One day, tired of wrestling with an unruly typewriter, she took the whole thing apart and reassembled it to operate to her satisfaction. Her aptitude at last revealed, the girl became not a stenographer, but the typewriter repairer for the school's business department.

"It's an old idea, this fitting people for life. The trouble is, we've forgotten it," Emily maintained.[13] An old idea, indeed, the very word *vocation* is derived from the Latin root meaning a "calling." Thomas Aquinas, thirteenth-century saint and theologian, asserted, "To live well is to work well, to display a good activity." Aquinas had no doubt that the Almighty predisposed people to particular occupations. "This division of various tasks among different persons is done by divine providence," he maintained, "inasmuch as some people are more inclined to one kind of work than to another."[14] In other words, a person's calling could be discovered in what he or she enjoyed and was equipped to do well. The idea of a vocational role, a functional relationship within society, fit perfectly with Emily's philosophy that educators should discover and develop each student's natural talent, preparing them for meaningful employment and a productive place in the community.

Studs Terkel, in his 1985 book *Working*, summed it up. He spoke of one's true vocation as "a search for daily meaning as well as daily bread, for recognition as well as cash…for a sort of life rather than a Monday through Friday sort of dying."

Opportunity School offered this chance to all who wished to learn. It was a hopeful alternative to daily disappointment, desperation, and demoralization. Viewed in that light, the only real surprise is that mere thousands reached for the brass ring held out by Emily Griffith. Enrollment swelled as the heartening news spread by word-of-mouth.

Emily's family life during the school's infant years was not uneventful. On December 19, 1917, Ethelyn R. Griffith married Evans J. Gurtner, a machinist and carpenter who also taught part-time at the Opportunity School. The bridegroom moved into the family home at 1524 Fillmore.[15]

This was, in fact, the second marriage for Emily's youngest sister. From 1904 until their divorce in 1914, Ethelyn had been Mrs. Herbert Willis. The 1910 Colorado census lists the Willises at the Fillmore address.

The Gurtners' marriage license presents a conundrum that, once solved, could illuminate many mysteries inherent in Emily Griffith's story. The 1885 Nebraska census listed Ethelyn Griffith as nine years old—eight years younger than Emily—indicating a birth year of 1876. But this is inconsistent with both the 1917 Gurtner marriage license, which lists her age as twenty-six, and her obituary, which gives her date of birth as 1891. On the basis of these two documents, Ethelyn would have been not eight, but twenty-three years younger than Emily.

Perhaps the Ethelyn Griffith born in 1876 did not survive into adulthood, and another child born in 1891 was named in the first daughter's memory. But if that were the case, why would Martha Griffith's obituary, which mentions a son, Warren, who died in infancy, neglect to include the death of the first Ethelyn? Equally curious is the fact that Ethelyn's obituary cites her birthplace as Cincinnati, Ohio. By 1891, the Griffith family had been homesteading in Nebraska for seven years. It is conceivable that the frail Martha chose to return to Ohio and stay with relatives or friends until her late-in-life baby was born.

The only certainty is that things don't add up. The 1910 Colorado census lists Ethelyn Willis as twenty-six, married six years. But seven years later, when she married again, she reported her age again as twenty-six. These documents suggest birth years of 1884 and 1891 respectively. Were she born in 1876, she would have been forty-one years old when she wed twenty-four-year-old Evans Gurtner. Were she born in 1891, she would have just turned thirteen when she married Herbert Willis. Apparently Emily was not the only Griffith sister to get creative with her age.

Another possibility begs consideration. In 1884, Emily Griffith was sixteen; in 1891, she was in her early twenties. Might she have found herself, as the result of either impetuous romance or unfortunate abuse, "in a family way," as it was then euphemistically described? She would not have been the only young woman in those times to disappear for several months with her mother and return with a new little sister.

Such a scenario would go a long way toward explaining why Emily almost never spoke of her experiences in Nebraska. It might also factor in to the decision to relocate to Colorado and the white lie about her age.

Nineteenth-century society considered women who bore children out of wedlock damaged goods. If Emily accepted this condemnatory characterization, it could explain her refusal of marriage proposals throughout her life. Her protestations about responsibility to Florence and her family may have masked a deep-seated feeling of unworthiness. Moreover, if her past did indeed hold the secret of such a mistake, the source of her fervent belief in everyone's right to second chances becomes obvious.

Regrettably, the Hamilton County archives at the University of Cincinnati contain no birth record whatsoever for Ethelyn R. Griffith. According to Suzanne Finck of the Archives and Rare Books Department, births in the county "were not required to be registered until 1895, and even then it was done haphazardly."[16] The collection of records was accessible to the public for nearly a century, leaving them vulnerable to pilfering, and they were exposed to floods and fire while housed in the Hamilton County Courthouse in the early 1900s.

Thus it may never be known for certain exactly when Ethelyn Griffith was born or to whom. A potentially pivotal episode of Emily Griffith's life must remain—at least for now and perhaps forever—entirely in the realm of speculation.

Emily's father, Andrew Griffith, passed away soon after Christmas 1918. When mine workers who had trained at the school heard of her loss, they visited her home and offered what little money they could to help her with funeral expenses. Her mother, Martha Craig Griffith, died on October 6, 1920. Martha had been keenly interested in the Opportunity School students, especially those who had no home of their own. Over the years, Mrs. Griffith "adopted" many of them, particularly boys in the service, and they called her Mother. She was eulogized thusly:

> Some men and women are known for great deeds they themselves perform; others will be known and called "Blessed" not for what they did, but for what they inspired others to do.[17]

Emily's parents were laid to rest in Denver's Fairmount Cemetery in the same Block 61 family plot where her own headstone would one day stand in her memory.

Evans Gurtner's name disappeared from the *Denver City Directory* for several years beginning in 1926. But Ethel continued to teach at Opportunity and to live in the Fillmore Street house with her sisters. Jeanne Varnell noted in her biographical sketch of Griffith for *Women of Consequence: The Colorado Women's Hall of Fame* that by turning down suitors throughout her life in deference to her family obligations and her career, this woman—who seemed to know what everyone else needed—may have shortchanged herself.

Establishing and launching the revolutionary institution that was Opportunity School were remarkable accomplishments. Keeping it operational in the social context of 1920s Denver would demand nothing less than heroic conviction.

6

Against the Current

"*Post* Charity Doesn't Care a Whoop about Race, Color or Creed," Frances Wayne declared in the headlines of her article pleading for donations. Not all in Denver shared her liberal perspective. As Emily Griffith helped "Pinky" refold clothing donated to the *Denver Post*'s annual Christmas drive in 1915, bold advertisements in that newspaper heralded the upcoming and long-awaited local premiere of a new film—by a very different Griffith—at the Tabor Grand. Advance publicity for D.W. Griffith's *Birth of a Nation* promised "It will make a better American of you." With matinee ticket prices beginning at 25 cents, almost anyone could afford to see it. But not everyone in Denver wanted it to be seen.

On December 13, 1915, the day after the premier, the *Denver Post* film critic reported "some preliminary skirmishing prior to its presentation." Protestors asserted that the film "presented the Negro in a wrong light and would injure his standing as a citizen." In response, city officials ordered a private preview be given to an invited crowd of one hundred, including a dozen "colored" men, a couple of clergymen, and two women who had joined the brouhaha. "At 7 o'clock the decision was reached that 'The Birth of a Nation' was unobjectionable; that it might go on," reported the reviewer. "Still, there were several who persisted it was undesirable."

The large opening night crowd, along with the critic, had found the film quite wonderful pictorially and enjoyed the entertainment immensely. All the fuss struck the *Post* reviewer as "scarcely tenable." The events portrayed happened during reconstruction fifty years earlier, he pointed out, when "as a matter of self-preservation, when conditions became unbearable, the Southern landowners formed the Ku Klux Klan and came into possession of their own. Why not?"

Those accustomed to pliant, courteous Negroes who tacitly accepted their subservient roles were taken aback by the depiction in *Birth of a Nation* of the black race as violent, ignorant, easily manipulated savages. "The Southern white understands how to manage [the Negro]," the reviewer concluded. "I think I know, because I have investigated."

Denver's Opportunity School had been operating for nearly five years when Klan Imperial Wizard William Joseph Simmons came to Denver in the spring of 1921. Simmons spoke to a select group of men at the prestigious Brown Palace Hotel. His audience was easily convinced of the rightness of his cause and was initiated on the spot into the so-called Denver Doers Club.[1]

In his book, *Hooded Empire,* Robert Goldberg explained the organization's appeal. "The Klan offered an attractive program of Americanism, militant Protestantism, fraternity, order, religious intolerance, and racial purity." Since Reconstruction, the "new" Klan had evolved into more of an equal opportunity hate group. In addition to blacks, they now reviled Jews, Catholics, and immigrants. The multifaceted platform of the 1920s KKK had something for nearly everyone.

More than 500,000 women augmented the ranks of the Klan nationwide. In Denver, Bishop Alma White of the Pillar of Fire Church considered Roman Catholicism a major obstacle to women's suffrage and equality. Additionally, the Klan supported Prohibition, thus making it "the foe of the twin evils enslaving women," according to White. Embracing the enemy of her enemies, the church leader beseeched her followers, "To whom shall we look to champion the cause and to protect the rights of women? Is there not evidence that the Knights of the Ku Klux Klan are the prophets of a new and better age?"[2]

The Klan tapped into the distrust and misunderstanding of foreign-born residents. Many Denver "natives" had come to feel invaded by these outsiders. Immigrants in general were construed as a threat to "pure Americanism" and suspected of "wanting only to siphon America's wealth and return to lives of ease in their homelands."[3]

The Italians of North Denver were accused of producing and distributing bootleg wine and whiskey, as well as drug trafficking. The Klan also capitalized on the "Catholic conspiracy" paranoia, contending that Roman Catholics placed their allegiance to the Pope above their loyalty to the United States and that they were plotting to take control of the government.

Klan influence magnified Denver's growing anti-Semitism. The city's Jewish population, centered around West Colfax Avenue, increased by 900 percent from 1916 to 1926. The alien nature of the area known as Little Jerusalem aroused suspicion and mistrust, giving rise to characterizations of Jews as "cagey and aggressive." Jews became linked in the minds of many Denverites with bootlegging and illicit gambling.[4]

Denver's 1920 population of 256,000 included only 6,175 blacks, but they were a vocal minority. In 1915, Denver blacks had organized the Colored Protection League, a branch of the National Association for the Advancement of Colored People (NAACP). They rebelled against their second-class citizenship by attempting to integrate theaters, school social events, and municipal recreational facilities. They were beginning to buy homes outside the Five Points ghetto in white neighborhoods, which made homeowners there uncomfortable and uneasy about their property values.[5]

As it did wherever it found a foothold, the Klan in Denver scratched at preexisting local irritations until they bled. Their success was solidly clinched when they merged their disparate grievances with demands for law and order. In 1921, Denver was plagued with lawlessness on many fronts. Though brothels and prostitution had been officially outlawed since 1913, lax enforcement of the ban had opened the way for more than sixty thriving houses. Likewise, in Colorado's fifth year of Prohibition, liquor was easily obtainable and cheap. Free samples of narcotics and other drugs were distributed at local high schools. Incidences of burglary, holdups, and murders had spiked. Arrests averaged 53 per day, totaling 19,649 for the year—a 28 percent increase over 1920.

Crime and arrest rates rose even further in 1922. Denver police were seen as corrupt and ineffectual. To many, the Klan appealed because it seemed the only organization capable of dealing with rampant crime and vice.

Under the leadership of Colorado's Grand Dragon Dr. John Galen Locke, the Klan played up the minority connection to crime and the city government's inability to solve Denver's problems. Before long, the KKK attracted sufficient support to begin effecting decisionmaking and political action at the local level.

Mayor Ben Stapleton was Klan member #1128 and a close friend of Locke's. Secretly supported by the Klan, Stapleton pledged a war on crime and inefficient government and won the mayoral election of 1923. With Stapleton's appointment of fellow Klansmen to key municipal government offices, the KKK dominated City Hall and the local police force. The Klan was above the law because, increasingly, the Klan *was* the law. Now protected from official retaliation, militancy was encouraged. Klansmen employed cross burnings, business boycotts, physical harassment, and death threats.

It is unlikely that Emily Griffith knew Dr. Locke, but she certainly knew about him. Her friend Frances Wayne interviewed Locke for an article that ran in the *Denver Post* August 14, 1924. She described a bloated, toadlike man sporting diamond rings, a stick pin, and watch fob, who hatched his machinations in a Glenarm Place office replete with antique weapons lining the walls and a guardian suit of armor.

"Looking at Dr. Locke," Wayne wrote, "it is not difficult to conclude why the form and circumstance, the pomp and ceremony of the Ku Klux Klan appealed to his imagination. His tastes are of another age."

Speaking of the Colorado Klan, Locke told Wayne, "Formed on militant lines, it has the added advantage of secrecy maintained by the uniform worn by the members. In secrecy resides the element of mystery; mystery shrouds strength and number and fear as well."

Locke broke the usual Klan rule of silence by publicly boasting of his organization's political influence to the press: "The Klan had charge of the [1923] campaign and election of Mayor Stapleton, and is entitled to credit for his overwhelming victory at the polls."

Wayne observed, "Dr. Locke speaks in a drawling voice. He doesn't seem enthusiastically interested. He doesn't have to be. If the Klan does not actually control the political situation in Colorado," she concluded, "it at least controls the balance of power."

Even the feisty *Denver Post*, which usually loved a fight, feared to take a stand against the Klan and its activities, lest it become "the lowest place on Champa Street."[6] Like the *Rocky Mountain News* and the *Denver Times,* the *Post's* position was inconsistent at best.

"Denver's inability to generate an effective counterforce during the Klan's formative years…facilitated the movement's expansion," according to Robert A. Goldberg in *The Invisible Empire in the West.* "Opinion makers—Protestant ministers, newspaper editors and other leading community figures—emitted ambiguous signals; most were unable and perhaps unwilling to define the Klan as deviant. In the vacuum of their silence, the secret society amassed men, money, and goodwill."[7]

At the outset of the 1924 statewide election campaign, Stapleton dropped all pretense, vowing, "I will work with the Klan and for the Klan in the coming election, heart and soul." That year, the KKK commandeered the Colorado Republican Party, securing "kleagle" (Klan-affiliated) nominees for every major office, including District Judge Clarence F. Morley for governor.

The other Republican gubernatorial candidate, former Lieutenant Governor Earl Cooley, took his defeat by the Klan political machine neither gracefully nor quietly. Cooley called the "Invisible Empire" a "sinister organization [which] entered our state for the sole purpose of creating turmoil, setting neighbor against neighbor, exciting class and social hatreds, [and] injecting religious intolerance into our political affairs."

On primary election day 1924, Klan members distributed "pink tickets" throughout Denver, listing every candidate for public office and designating each as Protestant, Catholic, or Jew. Protestants with an asterisk indicated a person deemed "unsatisfactory because of Roman Catholic affiliations and friendships."[8]

Colorado voters elected Klan members to the governor's office (Clarence Morley), the U.S. Senate seat (Rice Means), and scores of state legislative seats and county offices. Klansmen were elected lieutenant governor, auditor, attorney general, secretary of state, and Supreme Court justice. Their Republican party controlled both houses of the state legislature. Locke and the leaders of the Colorado Klan had every reason to consider the state in the palms of their 100 percent American hands.[9]

Emily Griffith's accomplishment of sustaining the Opportunity School is all the more heroic when viewed in this context. At a time when the popular and generally accepted thing to do was blame personal and societal problems on racial, ethnic, and religious minority groups, Griffith and her school sought instead to uplift the very groups that were the targets of discrimination.

When immigrants and their children were persecuted, stereotyped, or harassed, she held out a positive, compassionate model of what America could mean to would-be citizens. When blacks were thwarted in their every attempt to realize true equality, she made them believe by her example that one day others would recognize the righteousness of their ambitions.

The Colorado Klan's dark star blazed brightly, but briefly. It essentially burned out in seven months. The KKK knew how to seize power, but not how to wield it. The discovery that Grand Dragon Locke had not paid income taxes in years took the wind out of the Klan's lily-white sails and mired their leader in scandal and disgrace.

The Keith Boehm case provided another nail in the Klan coffin. The hapless nineteen-year-old East High student, a Klan member himself, was forcibly taken to Locke's office and compelled, under threat of castration, to marry a young woman several months pregnant. This was the break Klan opponents such as Denver District Attorney Phillip Van Cise and Judge Ben Lindsey had been waiting for. They filed kidnapping and conspiracy charges against Locke and made a public show of taking him into custody. The humiliating debacle made Locke the object of public ridicule and raised serious questions about not only his leadership, but also the Klan's vaunted respect for law and order.[10]

Mayor Stapleton, like so many other former affiliates, was quick to denounce the organization and distance himself from it. He never looked back. Even without Klan support, he served many more years in Denver public office. Upon his eighth run for mayor, Emily Griffith was actually featured in a newspaper plea to Opportunity School alumni to back Stapleton in May 1947.

The Klan was not alone in its opposition to the Opportunity School in its early years. Soon after the United States entered World War I, an arson plot against the school's facility was suspected. "Federal Agents Scent Plot at Local Trade School," read the *Denver Post* headline on June 24, 1917. "Infernal Machine is Found in Instructional Room of Red Cross...Pro-German is Blamed."

The highly speculative and unsubstantiated report intimated that parts of a possible incendiary device had been found beneath a school fire escape. The building's night janitor had heard noises from an upper floor—"someone stirring papers"—soon after midnight. When he went to investigate, the culprit escaped unseen through a third-story window. Bandage drawers in the Red Cross training room were found ajar, but nothing else was disturbed.

From this scant evidence, U.S. Secret Service agent Rowland K. Goddard built "a plot by a fanatic with pro-German sympathies to blow up or [set] fire [to] the Opportunity School, where a class of 60 persons is taking daily instructions in Red Cross first aid work." Further, "It is believed that his aim was to interfere with instruction, perhaps set machines which would explode when the room was filled with students."[11] No basis was cited for this conclusion, nor did a single follow-up story ever run.

Far more substantial was the threat posed to the Opportunity School by Bricklayers Union #1 of Colorado in 1923. While the union's traditional apprenticeship program took three years, an improvised hands-on training program in the school's basement was turning out qualified masons in only three months. School board member F. H. Cowell, in the building trades himself, received an ultimatum from the union's secretary, expressing strenuous objection to this circumvention of their rules and

informing him that if Opportunity continued to teach other than inden-
tured apprentices, "union bricklayers will be unable to man your work."[12]

To his credit, Cowell refused to ask school board colleagues to
shut down the abbreviated program he considered to be in the public
interest. Union bricklayers, making good on their threat, walked off
his jobs in strike. Fittingly, it was with the help of Opportunity
School students that Cowell was able to finish his contracts
nonetheless.

The ugly episode clearly demonstrated to Principal Griffith that
union leaders did not take being bypassed lightly. She responded by
making every effort thenceforth to work in cooperation with organized
labor groups. Suggestions of the Carpenters' Union were implemented
with the establishment of an advanced carpentry course taught by
master carpenters, complete with a union-approved apprenticeship.
Similar working partnerships with the unions for plumbers, electricians, and commercial bakers soon followed.

No one, however well-intentioned, successfully challenges the
status quo without making some enemies. By empowering minorities
and immigrants through education, Emily Griffith undoubtedly
enraged the small-minded members of Denver's Ku Klux Klan. By
pioneering more efficient methods of vocational training, she ran afoul
of at least one powerful labor union. What is impossible to know is
how many individuals she may have alienated by offering previously
exploited women the means to take care of themselves.

Countless turn-of-the-century women in Denver, as elsewhere,
found themselves in demoralizing, degrading, even life-threatening
circumstances, largely as the consequence of limited options. Perhaps
they were trapped in abusive marriages because they had no way to
provide for themselves and their children. Perhaps they were ignorant
and unschooled because they had had to go to work quite young, or
because their parents had seen no value in educating girls. Perhaps they
had fallen into prostitution because they had been sexually abused,
lacked self-esteem, or considered the work somehow preferential to
other forms of exploitation. Perhaps they worked at grueling,

demeaning, or hazardous menial labors that sapped both their strength and their spirits.

To such women, Emily Griffith's Opportunity School was a boon. Education and vocational training were the keys to their liberation. It could mean their independence.

Men who had built themselves up by tearing these women down—be they husbands, ex-lovers, supervisors, or pimps—were threatened by this independence. What they could not control and thus could not tolerate was the woman who had tasted hope, who had found an alternative to her desperation, who had newfound confidence and courage to leave destructive relationships behind and strike out on her own.

Then, as now, petty tyrants who derived satisfaction or profited from the mistreatment of others were known to employ violence, to retaliate irrationally, and to nurse grudges. Today's news is still rife with reports of estranged boyfriends or ex-husbands who cold-bloodedly murder women they feel they can no longer claim or control.

Despite such dangers engendered by empowerment, Emily Griffith was not detoured by fear or intimidation. She stayed the course, believing in the legitimacy of her mission and in the fundamental dignity of all who made their way onboard.

In her personal files,[13] Emily kept a poem entitled "The Test" by George W. Olinger, which seemed to express her own philosophy:

> It's the bumps you get and the jolts you get
>   And the shocks that your courage stands,
> The hours of sorrow and vain regret,
>   The prize that escapes your hands,
> That test your mettle and prove your worth;
>   It isn't the blows you deal,
> But the blows you take on this good old earth
>   That shows if your stuff is real.

An Emily Griffith Scrapbook

Courtesy Colorado Historical Society 96.223.16

Sisters Emily, Ethelyn, and Florence in an undated photograph.

Denver Post, June 19, 1947

Earliest known photo of Emily K. Griffith, most likely from her teaching years in Nebraska.

Courtesy Colorado Historical Society 96.223.20

Emily's parents, Andrew and Martha Griffith, on the steps of the family home at 1524 Fillmore, Denver.

Ethelyn (Ethel) Gurtner, Emily's youngest sister.

"She was always smiling at you. And when her hand touched yours, you knew she had great sincerity and a warm heart."
— Opportunity Student Alferd Adamo

Many of the photographs left by Emily were undated and unlabeled. Someone other than Emily labeled this photograph "Emily's sweetheart."

❧ ✦ ❧

These students were probably one of Emily's classes at the Central or Twenty-fourth Street School

Children Aided by Big Brothers Give Ten Pennies to Aid Others

Little Boy and Girl Show Their Gratitude as Best They Can.

Every Mail Is Full of Christmas Appeals From Waifs.

BIG BROTHERS FUND.	
Previously acknowledged	$2,076.75
J. C. D. Girls' club	5.00
A Business Woman	10.00
Big Brother	1.00
Mrs. D. L. Dickinson	5.00
Two Friends	.75
Mrs. Carl R. Neuser	2.00
Harriet A. Myers	10.00
O. H. Parr	1.00
A Big Sister	.50
Oscar (5 years old)	.20
A Friend	1.00
A Friend	.25
A Big Sister	1.00
A Big Brother	.25
Big Sister	1.00
J. L. Parker	3.10
A Big Sister	1.00
Harry and Charlotte Shaffer	.10
A Big Sister	1.00
Two Little Brothers (Rocky Ford)	.50
Sherman School Children (Madrid, Iowa)	1.25
A 3-year-old Little Brother	.50
A Friend (Vernal, Utah)	7.00
Dick Richardson (Folsom, N. M.)	2.00
A Big Brother (Hugo, Colo.)	5.00
Miscellaneous Contributions	6.30

(By FRANCES WAYNE.)

Charlotte and Henry Shaffer came to the office of the Big Brother editor yesterday and donated a dime to the Big Brothers fund. This little boy and girl had been helped by the Big Brothers.

Harry and Charlotte Shaffer, as they looked after being fitted out with clothes and shoes by The Post Big Brother Fund. They walked from their home to The Post this morning and then gave their carfare to the Big Brother Fund.

<u>Denver Post</u>, Christmas charity drive, December 12, 1915

<u>Denver Post</u> reporter Frances "Pinky" Wayne met and befriended Emily Griffith during the 1915 Big Brothers Christmas Drive. She used her influence to promote the Opportunity School.

Courtesy Western History Department, Denver Public Library

REORGANIZED BOARD AUTHORIZES OPPORTUNITY SCHOOL FOR DENVER

Directors Transact Important Business During Short Session—Miss Emily Griffith to Be Principal Of New Educational Feature.

Denver Post May 12, 1916

An early picture of Opportunity School faculty. Miss Griffith valued understanding and compassion over formal education in her teachers.

Courtesy the Tom Noel Collection

The automobile course was popular with both men and women.

The school also offered classes in masonry and millinery.

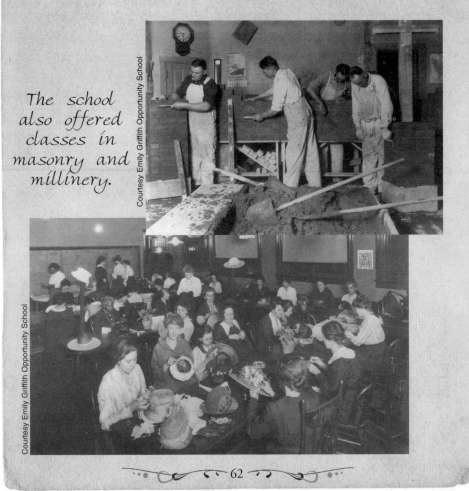

Courtesy Emily Griffith Opportunity School

Courtesy Emily Griffith Opportunity School

NEW 'OPPORTUNITY SCHOOL' TO TEACH BUSINESS TO PUPILS

MISS EMILY GRIFFITH
Progressive Denver School Teacher, Who Is Popularly Known as "the Little Mother of the Twenty-fourth Street School." She Will Shortly Establish an "Opportunity School," Where the Young or Old, Men or Women, May Drop in at Almost Any Hour of the Day or Night and Get Practical Training in Whatever Line Interests Them.

Young and Old Will Be Told How to Find and Hold Jobs.

The Opportunity school will co-operate with all the business men of Denver. We will ask the business men's suggestions as to what training a boy or girl ought to have...

Everything One Wants to Know About Earning Living Taught.

Denver Post, May 14, 1916

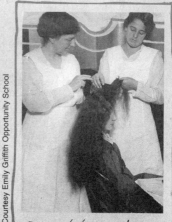

Beautician Class

Cobbler class.

Business and salesmanship classes applied to many careers.

ONE LITTLE WOMAN GIVES OPPORTUNITY TO 1,500 PUPILS

Unusual Denver School Attracts Attention of Educators Over U. S.

USEFUL LIVING TAUGHT

The... DENVER KIWANIAN

Vol. XXIII   Wednesday, June 26, 1946   No. 26

ALBANY HOTEL
Cathedral Room—12 Noon-1:30 P. M.

A Rose for Emily Griffith

Today we inscribe our meeting to the honor of the only woman member of Kiwanis, a member of our Denver Club since 1920,—Miss Emily Griffith. She is a born builder. Under the inspiration of her spirit, vision, and work, the Emily Griffith Opportunity School was founded "for All who wish to learn." Out of her kindling suggestion, No. 9 Pearl Street, a home for homeless boys, was established. Her heart, as large as humanity, her generous, creative spirit, quickened the soul of Denver to high achievements. Because of its power to inspire, we keep the memory of what she has done vivid. Because the way she pointed is now so clearly essential, we walk in it with increasing purpose. And so today, a rose for Emily Griffith, a token of our love for her, and of our faith in her vision.

CHEATED
out of
A Home, An Education *and*
A Chance to Make Good

but
No. 9 PEARL STREET
is on the Job

The Denver Kiwanis Club sponsored No. 9 Pearl Street, "A home for the boy who needs one."

1946 program from the Tribute to Emily by the Denver Kiwanis Club.

Rocky Mountain News, February 10, 1927

MEN NEEDN'T FEAR WOMEN IN BUSINESS, CLUB IS TOLD

Emily in the living room of her Pinecliffe cabin where she lived following retirement in 1933.

EMILY GRIFFITH QUITS TEACHING

Famous Educator, Founder of Opportunity School, Retires

Miss Emily Griffith, one of the most widely known and best beloved educators in Colorado, retired yesterday from the active duties to which she has devoted a quarter of a century of her life.

Founder of Denver's famous Opportunity School and its principal during the more than 17 years of its existence, Miss Griffith is nationally known among educators and particularly among those interested in adult education work.

Many of the nation's foremost school authorities have come here to study Miss Griffith's work. Numerous other cities have used her Opportunity School as a model for adult educational activities.

The cabin kitchen where murder investigators on June 19, 1947 found dinner prepared for three.

AN APPEAL TO
OPPORTUNITY SCHOOL
GRADUATES

BY
EMILY GRIFFITH

*Emily Griffith,
circa 1920.*

Emily Griffith, founder and for many years principal of Denver's Opportunity School—which has brought renown to Denver throughout this and other nations—says that without the help and encouragement which Mayor Stapleton gave to her, it is doubtful if Opportunity School could have won its present unique place of leadership in the educational world. More than 200,000 people from all walks of life have graduated from this school and have gone on to useful careers as a result of the training they received in this world-famous institution. Miss Griffith says:

"Today there are many thousands of successful men and women in Denver who owe their success to Opportunity School. I appeal now to these men and women who will cast their ballots at the election Tuesday, May 20. I want to make it plain to them, if they do not know it already, that they owe a deep debt of gratitude to Mayor Stapleton. I remember when my program at Opportunity School was threatened by a clique of politicians, and how deeply grateful I was for the friendship and loyalty of my former students. Now Ben Stapleton is faced with a combination of politicians who would undo much of the splendid work he has fostered. With all my heart I want to appeal to the tens of thousands of former students of Opportunity School to show that they are grateful for his loyal and enthusiastic support during the years when they were seeking and gaining opportunity. They can show this gratitude and loyalty by going to the polls on May 20 and casting their ballots for the warm-hearted and far-seeing public official who has helped make Opportunity School possible—Ben F. Stapleton!"

The people of Denver are proud of the great work for humanity accomplished by Opportunity School—and they are proud of Emily Griffith, for her enterprise and courage in creating an educational institution that has been copied all over the world!

ELECT
BEN STAPLETON
TUESDAY, MAY 20

*Rocky Mountain News,
May 14, 1947*

The Business and Professional
Women's Club of Denver
Incorporated

1932
WOMAN OF THE YEAR AWARD

Presented to

Emily Griffith

Upon the occasion of
National Business Women's Week

Given at Denver, Colorado, this Eighth day of March,
One thousand nine hundred and thirty-two...

Bessie M. Jones
President

Famous Educator And Sister Are Found Slain At Pinecliffe

JUN 1 9 1947

Camera JUN 1 9 1947

Rocky Mountain News,
front page, June 20, 1947

 Rocky Mountain News

86TH YEAR: NO. 171   DENVER, COLO, FRIDAY JUNE 20, 1947   PHIL...

'MERCY' MOTIVE IN KILLING OF EMILY GRIFFITH

EMILY GRIFFITH—Her Last Picture

By PASQUALE MARRANZINO
Rocky Mountain News Writer
Copyright 1947, by The Denver Publishing Co.

PINECLIFFE, June 19.—Boulder County sheriff's officers and Denver police tonight speculated that the bizarre double slaying of Emily Griffith, famed Denver educator, and her invalid sister, Florence, might prove to be mercy killings.

Piecing together a handful of meager clues, the officers instituted a nation-wide search for kindly, quiet, 61-year-old Fred Wright Lundy, who 29 years ago taught under Emily Griffith in the world-famous Opportunity School she founded.

Lack of Motives Baffling

Baffled by a lack of motives for the shocking slayings, officers theorized that the recluse and inventor had taken the lives of the aged sisters with whom he had seen in almost constant company in this mountain hamlet for the past 13 years.

Neighbors and friends of the sisters and Lundy pointed out that Florence Griffith in the past year had become an increasingly heavy burden in the life of Emily Griffith. She had been in ill health for many years and recently had shown signs of failing fast.

Felt Emily Was 'Martyr'

Lundy, they said, on many occasions had expressed grief over the "martyr" life which Emily had spent in caring for her sister. On occasions he expressed the sentiment that he would rather "see them dead than the way they are living."

Dick Griffith, petroleum geologist and a nephew of the Griffith sisters, asserted that he believed "Fred decided it

(Continued on Page 3)

My Memories of Emily Griffith

By Her Closest Friend for 30 Years
FRANCES WAYNE
—Page 14

First Murder Scene Pictures
—A full page on Page 16

Magnificent Obsession
—The Story of Emily Griffith's Grand Idea on Page 6

67

Dear Lois Dick, Rusty.

Just a few days ago I received a photo of Rusty, the most happy intelligent, & perfect boys Photo I ever saw. Every one who sees it want to hug him. Right now he is looking at me & seems to say "What do you know about this shirt? Now I shall have to make you all a visit when you locate in Melica. You will get lots of new thrills at such an interesting place. We are - all well, Florence sits and looks at ~~Dick~~ Rusty with the most satisfied & happy expression, Ethel & Emily are just too thrilled for words & we thank you more than we can say. Love

Emily

Mailed the day she died, Emily's last letter was to her nephew and his family.

Griffith Sisters' Rites Marked by Simplicity

The Griffith sisters' memorial service was held at Central Presbyterian Church in Denver. A steady rain did not deter the more than 300 mourners from all sectors of the community.

My Memories of Emily Griffith

By Frances Wayne
(Emily Griffith's closest friend for 30 years)

EMILY GRIFFITH is dead! Oh, no she isn't nor ever will be.

Emily Griffith, the gentle woman whose life was that of a happy child, whose faith in human nature had no bounds, whose one thought was to be helpful to those in need of help over the rough ways of life, is so far as the flesh is concerned said to be dead.

Emily Griffith, the woman, who gave a new meaning to education and to the lives of thousands of boys and girls, men and women, will never die. I make this assured statement out of the experience of a long, close, cherished friendship kept aglow through the years by a profound reverence for her character, ideals and simplicity.

One of the world's great women, she lacked self-pride, but possessed those qualities of heart and soul which made a certain Man of Galilee the object of veneration to his companions and of the ages.

* * *

I FIRST knew Emily Griffith when many years ago at the Christmas season she came to my newspaper office to ask a favor for the pupils of the Twenty-Fourth Street School, located then in one of Denver's poorer districts. As she examined the clothing and trinkets contributed by interested citizens, she said, "I wonder if you will let me tell you of a hope I have for the people in and out of my school—the boys and girls, their parents, too; whose education has been limited by poverty?

"I want to help to establish a school where the clock will be stopped from morning until midnight. I want the age limit for admission lifted and the classes so organized that a boy or girl working in a bakery, store, laundry or any kind of a shop who has an hour or two to spare may come to school, study what he or she wants to learn to make life more useful.

"The same rule goes for older folks too. I know I will be laughed at, but what of it?" she asked with one of her bright smiles. "I already have a name for that school. It is Opportunity."

ACROSS the table piled with gifts, Emily Griffith and I shook hands and she agreed to go to work to procure such a school for Denver, ultimately for the country and far lands.

The day she was to present her new idea to the Denver Board of Education, she admitted, "I'm trembling like a leaf because perhaps I am too ambitious. For myself, I really want nothing."

Asked what she would expect in the way of a salary advance if permitted to organize such a school, she said, "I would expect no more than I am receiving as principal of Twenty-Fourth Street School because this is just an experiment."

So Denver's Opportunity School became a fact. Its founder, following her modest way, meeting with the courage of a brave spirit the opposition of old-line educators, holding no resentment against those who placed obstacles in her way, revealed loyalty as true as sunlight to those who had encouraged her to go forward.

"I'll go through fire and floods and even risk life for those who have been my friends," was one of the last statements made by this Christ-like woman to this writer as recently as May 15.

And so, Emily Griffith remained at her post and then went to a humble cabin home in Pinecliffe to live, when under the rule of the school she was retired to live on a school pension.

At the zenith of her fame as founder of Opportunity School, Emily Griffith received invitations from the governments of Russia, France, Germany and Great Britain to be a guest and personally direct the establishment in those lands of comparable schools. "What would I do so far from home?" She would ask with a laugh and turn to the task at hand.

* * *

LOCAL service clubs revered Emily Griffith and one, the Denver Kiwanis Club, named her "Sweetheart," and made sure that in her mountain home she did not lack comforts.

Emily Griffith learned the meaning of life by giving hers to others. She might have married but put that temptation aside to remain with an ailing mother.

"All right, Emily Griffith, take the place you have earned." This is the demand of one of your oldest, closest, most loving of friends who found no flaw in you or your life because you had reached as near perfection as a human may go.

<u>Rocky Mountain News</u>, June 20, 1947.

Emily and Florence's gravestone in Denver's Fairmount Cemetery bears no dates of birth.

Courtesy Joyce Lohse

EMILY GRIFFITH
JUNE 18, 1947
Founder Opportunity School
"For all who wish to learn"
FLORENCE GRIFFITH

FRED W. LUNDY.

Murder suspect Fred Lundy as he appeared on the front page of the Denver Post, June 19, 1947.

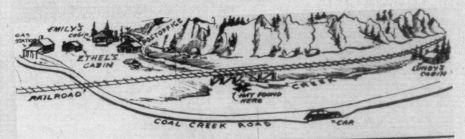

THIS SKETCH MAP, drawn by Post Staff Artist Angelo O'Dorisio, shows the Pinecliffe area where Miss Emily Griffith and her invalid sister, Florence, were shot to death late Wednesday.

Fred Lundy's cabin today.

Courtesy Debra Faulkner

*Emily Griffith
Opportunity
School in its
early years
and today.*

*More than one-and-a-half
million students have
passed through the doors
of EGOS seeking to
improve their lives.*

7
New Channels

"We represented cafeteria in education." Emily Griffith borrowed the metaphor used by a distinguished visitor to describe her Opportunity School concept to the National Education Association (NEA)'s 1926 convention. "Here is the thing spread out. Now come along—take what you want. You know it isn't quite as good a meal as you would get...in your high school, but it is a filling meal—that kind of education that gets them by in their days' work. It makes a happier look come into their eyes; it gives them the thing that they have been longing for.

"When the lights at the school go out, and we have been there since half-past-seven in the morning, and you see [the students] pass by...you see in the eyes of those people that there is something that is coming into their lives—a bigger and broader and fuller understanding."[1]

Opportunity's veritable smorgasbord of course offerings continued to expand and diversify throughout the school's first decade, as did the "diners." Classes were added in vulcanizing, salesmanship, advertising, electrical and acetylene welding, architectural drafting, bookbinding, shoe repair and cobbling, among many others. The school was so popular that in the second year, Opportunity had to begin limiting enrollment. Those who needed classes for employment were given priority. Rapid growth, particularly in the vocational fields, found representatives of the general business community, as well as such groups as barbers, bakers, and plumbers, assisting in devising training programs. Countless businessmen and women contributed their efforts and expertise to advisory committees, meeting periodically to update instructional methods and materials.

Opportunity alumni and other persons with useful skills donated their time as instructors. Hundreds of anonymous citizens contributed money and equipment to the school, which also depended upon the public to provide "live" projects for certain training programs, such as large and small appliance repair, automobile repair, and upholstery. Minimal fees were charged to community members brave enough to submit to barbering, hairstyling, or manicure practice. Donations of all sorts to the school store were gratefully accepted.

Principal Griffith initially resisted the addition of a high school program, chiefly because she didn't consider a secondary diploma essential for obtaining gainful employment. After all, she herself had done quite well without one. After the war, however, it became apparent that students in fields such as nursing and engineering could not continue in the positions they'd held in wartime without completing high school work. An accredited alternative high school program was initiated at Opportunity in 1919. Now student attendance and grades in required coursework had to be tracked and reported to Denver Public Schools. Emily soon realized that high school classes filled an important need for dropouts who wished to complete their neglected education and for high school graduates who needed a review before beginning post-secondary studies. The first Opportunity high school class graduated in 1923.

The roster for teacher Effie M. Cline's 1919 high school class at Opportunity lists 44 students ranging in age from 14 to 31; more than three-fifths of them were denoted simply as "21+." Surnames such as Kolchenver, Bielski, Herscheid, McGill, Sakujis, and Saisalina reflected the multicultural makeup of the group. The instructor carefully recorded marks of completion for Algebra, English IX, X, and XI, Ancient History, Medieval and Modern History, Geometry, Jr. High School Math, and General Science. Her personal comments followed each student's record:

"Dropped—Mother ill"
"Took millinery course"
"Went to [sugar] beet fields"
"An interesting lad"
"Present a few days one month"
"Attended four days"
"Hungarian—is good student"[2]

Cline's observations and careful attention to the circumstances of each individual under her tutelage were representative of the conscientiousness required of every Opportunity teacher. Miss Griffith's faculty meetings were brief and succinct. Her message was unmistakable: "No one in this school is supposed to frown," she declared. "Anyone of the staff who is heard to speak a harsh word is subject to immediate dismissal. Nor is a teacher permitted to call attention to a student's weaknesses. Many people have been ridiculed in other classrooms. Here we try to make them happy, believing that when they are happy, they are interested and want to learn."[3]

Hers was no mere rhetoric—"I would take a teacher with a high school certificate rather than a Master's degree, if she has understanding," she said. She once overheard an instructor say to a student, "I just don't understand how you can have reached your age without learning this."[4] Though hired only a few hours earlier, that teacher was let go on the spot.

"The mood which a teacher takes to her work is a measure of its success or failure," Griffith asserted. "I have enthusiasm for my work because I have a love for it."[5] She insisted upon—and got—the same from her staff. For example, there existed for many years a keen but friendly rivalry between the teachers in the commercial department of the school, who vied to see who could generate the most interest in his or her courses by offering extra assistance outside of class time and even over the telephone.

Griffith often used folksy sayings or proverbs to express her philosophy of teaching. "Help thy brother's boat across and lo, thine own has reached the shore"; "A stone fitted for a place in the wall does not stay long in the ditch"; and "By their joy ye shall know them."

She was a great proponent of "success practice" in instruction. "Give a pupil an assignment he can do so he will have a sense of joy and accomplishment," she recommended before challenging a student with completely new material.[6]

Emily graciously gave credit where credit was due. "This school drew to it teachers for whom no day was too long, or no problem too deep. Their contributions can never be overstated," she said in a *Denver Post* guest editorial many years after her retirement.[7] The admiration was mutual. "There never was a school where one could find his work so worthwhile," one teacher testified, "especially in meeting the unusual problems."

"Miss Griffith's unselfish stand is an inspiration to us to give ourselves as fully as she does," declared another. "Miss Griffith always makes you feel she appreciates your work when you are trying to do the best you can," stated a third. Yet another told the *Colorado School Journal* writer, "Miss Griffith is a peach to work for."

"Many a time have we at Opportunity School seen the outward change which bespoke the inner lifting of spirit," testified a teacher when asked about Miss Griffith's influence on staff and students.[8]

What most impressed the reporter for *Municipal Facts,* who wrote of "Denver's Famous Education Factory" in 1926, was the school's considerate treatment of every individual, regardless of age, sex, color, nationality, or previous education. With each prospective student, he observed, Opportunity staff "analyzes his strengths and weaknesses and classifies him accordingly—in that spirit of kindness and personal interest which bonds the student to the school at once, and imbues him instantly with earnestness and eagerness."[9]

In the same way that the school had mobilized before WWI to prepare enlistees for various types of war work, it rededicated its effort into postwar self-sufficiency training and vocational retraining of more than 400 returning wounded armed services veterans. Students were given the chance to develop their abilities, regardless of their disabilities.

Special accommodations were made to their instruction, enabling a paraplegic to learn watch repair or a blind man to become an electrician.

Classes in home economics, childcare, retail sales, beauty work, telephone switchboard operations, and clerical skills remained popular with female students. At the same time, Opportunity continued to pioneer the training of women for careers in nontraditional, higher-paying occupations such as dentistry, automechanics, welding, electrical trades, and business management.

Women's roles in the workplace were expanding and evolving. In 1927, Mrs. Helen Bell—Opportunity School alumnae, chairperson of the Women's Bureau of the Denver Chamber of Commerce, and public relations officer for Mountain States Telephone and Telegraph Company—addressed a meeting of the Denver Kiwanis Club to assure them, "You need not be afraid that the woman in business is trying to take your place. [She is] gradually carving a niche of her own."

Bell proceeded to characterize the three major types of women formerly employed in business: the female by whom "tears were used as a weapon and a defense of her errors," the "rouged and frilled vamp," and the "mannish, hard-boiled business type."

"The modern business woman," Mrs. Bell explained, "is trying to live down the impressions left by these early types. But give us about 15 years and bear with us in our difficulties," she implored the businessmen's association, "and women will have made themselves a necessary part of the business world." In closing, she confided, "Many a business woman feels that she could best 'express herself' in beaten biscuits and embroidery, but economic necessity forbids it."[10]

Opportunity was not only making strides against the racism and sexism of the day, but also making headway countering ageism—another issue of personal importance to Emily Griffith. "Years don't matter if you actually have the urge to learn," she insisted.[11]

"After two years' trial, we have satisfied ourselves that one does not need to be young to negotiate the educational grade successfully," she declared in 1919. "We have learned from experience that men and women past twenty-five years of age, knowing exactly what they want, make better students than the youngsters, because they are capable of thinking through a subject instead of relying on memory…[Older students] are there because they want to be. They are fitting themselves to meet the requirements of the work or business or profession they have elected to follow."[12]

Years later, she cited the example of older men enrolled in the school's popular cobbling classes. "Many of them have been laid off from their supposed lifetime jobs because their employers considered they were too old," Griffith told the *Denver Post* in 1930. "But these men still have ambitions to be self-supporting and to keep up their morale. They learn to be shoemakers and they are able to shift again for themselves independently."[13]

Age was a taboo topic with Miss Griffith, one of the few things she did not discuss. "I never tell my age," she'd say dismissively, if pressed. "It's all right for men. But it's different for women. Somehow it dates them."[14] She forfeited her chance to be included in a volume of *Who's Who in Education* because the biographical submission form included date of birth. Emily claimed that even her sisters did not know how old she was.

The secret of personal backdating on her initial Denver Public Schools application must have weighed vaguely upon her conscience. Opportunity's every demonstration of the trainability and continued usefulness of older graduates was something of a personal affirmation for this woman who had undertaken the educational enfranchisement of adults when she herself was fifty.

Emily's friend, reporter Frances Wayne, rushed to her defense in 1919 when DPS Superintendent Carlos Cole and other members of the school board attempted to take credit for the success of the school. "A flagrant larceny," Pinky called it. "There is one thing the people of Denver should see to," she declared. "That the credit of originating, founding, [and] developing the Opportunity School shall not be wrested from Miss Emily Griffith."[15]

In 1924, the Denver school board considered closing the school for economic reasons. Three school board members—Hallett,

Schenck, and Taylor—successfully fought to save it, pointing out that Opportunity's annual boost to the city and state economies was estimated to be in the millions of dollars. That year alone, it counted 9,000 enrollments and more than 32,000 graduates.

Begun in two classrooms of the old Longfellow School, Opportunity had long ago taken over the entire building. Obliged to keep pace with the school's ever-expanding enrollment and course offerings, the Denver School Board finally authorized new facilities be added to the 13th and Welton street site. The new building, a four-story structure at the opposite end of the block, was erected in 1926.

One of the most important components of the Opportunity School venture was its Employment Bureau, established in 1928. Miss Griffith's network of business contacts proved once again instrumental to the success of this aspect of the school's services. Employers posted part-time positions for students, who had to earn while they learned. Upon completing vocational courses, students could look to the school's employment bureau for referrals or placement in full-time opportunities that utilized their new skills. Some found jobs for the first time, thanks to knowledge gained at Opportunity; others earned promotions or transitioned into more satisfying careers as the result of skills acquired there.

The bureau soon evolved into the school's Employment Adjustment Service, which went beyond mere employment placement. It followed up on every Opportunity graduate who found work, making sure he or she had everything necessary for continued success on the job, from skills to professional wardrobe, transportation arrangements, and even adequate daily nutrition.

The Depression called for new strategies to meet the needs of Denver's citizens and employers. Many companies sent their employees to the school for several hours a day to improve various job-related skills. Conversely, Opportunity sometimes dispatched its teachers off-site to offer instruction in the workplace. Sales clerks employed by Daniels & Fisher, Joslins, Denver Dry Goods, and other downtown department stores were taught fractions and percentages to help them measure out fabrics or calculate sale discounts. Employees of Gates Rubber Company received on-the-job instruction in vulcanization. Classes in telegraphy were conducted for railroad employees at Union Station.

During the Depression years, new types of training were in greater demand. Former waitresses, chambermaids, and sales clerks were obliged to take up unfamiliar trades. In the early 1930s, artificial flower making took the place of traditional floral design. Bookkeeping, typewriting, and shorthand classes reported the largest enrollments, closely followed by beauty parlor trade, acetylene and electrical welding, English for foreigners, and lip-reading for the deaf. A course entitled "Mend the Run in Silk Stockings" attracted 124 students in academic 1930–1931.

One creative contingent of citizens, harkening back to the state's "Pike's Peak or Bust" days of 1859 when a lucky few struck it rich with minimal investment, requested Opportunity classes in gold panning. Principal Griffith sought out the most literate old prospector available and assigned him the teaching task, then sent the group down to the Platte River and Cherry Creek in hopes of repeating history. Despite their optimism, no second gold rush materialized.

In the fall of 1930, Emily Griffith and her Opportunity School instructors announced their own war on illiteracy in Denver. A citywide canvas conducted by the office of Katherine L. Craig, state superintendent of public instruction and Emily's former boss, identified 4,000 citizens as illiterate. "As a progressive, forward-looking community, I think we should feel a bit shame-faced at being credited with even a few illiterates," Miss Griffith remarked in a September 7, 1930, *Denver Post* story. "Customarily, a person is rated as 'literate' if he can write his name and read even the most elemental sentences. I don't believe that is enough. A literate person ought to be able to read and write at least as well as a second or third grade pupil, I should think."

Opportunity's teachers volunteered to personally contact and recruit each and every one of those identified by Miss Craig's survey within the next two years, the article stated. "I am confident our Opportunity school could teach these 4,000 persons sufficient knowledge in three months to class them well above the minimum literacy level," the principal told the *Post*.

Before the 1930-1931 school year even began, the school was on track to exceed by several hundred its previous enrollment record of 9,500 for the academic year. One hundred and five faculty now taught forty-four occupational courses, as well as citizenship and English classes and general education courses to an army of adults. Thirty of those courses were funded in part by the federal Smith-Hughes Act for vocational training.

"Miss Griffith is a firm believer in a means of livelihood as a builder of individual morale," the 1930 *Post* article declared. "No family can keep up its morale and general faith in things if it can't have work to earn the daily bread," she said, "One of the greatest joys for every teacher here is the fact that the school teaches new occupations to so many adults so that they can find work and keep up their love of life."[16]

Opportunity's classes in welding during this period were acknowledged to be among the finest in the nation. Within a few months after completing the course, graduates could earn an average of $450 a month. *Fusion Facts,* a technical trade publication of the 1930s, reported, "Students are taught the sheer fundamentals of welding, without regard to any shape or form of tool or implement which may be welded. [A student is taught] not only flat work, but vertical and over-head…with either hand, forward or backward…corners where he must use a mirror to see what is going on. Obviously, a man with these tricks can weld most anything. The student [also] studies chemistry, physics, metallurgy and metallography. There is no guesswork with an Opportunity trained student. He must know beforehand whether or not the welding job will be a success."[17]

Opportunity's principal, too, garnered accolades throughout this period. In 1920, Emily Griffith was appointed to the State Child Welfare Board. The Colorado Education Association (CEA) elected her its president in 1922. She was appointed to the Board of Control

81

of the State Industrial School for Boys in 1924. When invited by the governments of Russia, Greece, Germany, England, and other nations to set up schools abroad along Opportunity's lines, she invariably chose to remain in Denver, serving the "folks" nearest her heart. "Several other cities have modeled schools on ours," Griffith noted in the early 1930s, "but Denver's Opportunity School still is the foremost of all. I really believe it takes a city like Denver, with generous, helpful citizens of its type, to make such an institution a success."[18]

Frances Wayne's paper, the *Denver Post*, staunchly supported Griffith and her efforts throughout the years and, in December 1931, mounted a campaign to award her Colorado motor vehicle License Plate #1, designating her as the state's Most Useful Citizen. She was presented with the license and displayed it on her car, which was probably a gift from the school's automotive training shop. In subsequent years, however, *Post* editor Fred Bonfils awarded Plate #1 to himself or his daughter, Helen.

By 1933, Denver's now internationally famous school had graduated 135,369 students of every age, of both genders, of every social class and of myriad races and nationalities. It consistently sent an average of 2,000 trained and qualified workers into the greater community every month. Against substantial odds, Emily Griffith had realized her lifelong ambition of creating a place "for all who wish to learn"—an endeavor imitated, though rarely equaled, throughout the nation and the world.

"I believe the highest calling a woman can have, besides being a homemaker, is to be a teacher," she said of her chosen profession. "Teaching other people's children is the only compensation we have, who have none of our own."[19]

By choice, Emily Griffith never married or raised a family. Opportunity was her "baby." But it was by no means an only child.

8

Tributaries

They knew they were in trouble. Boys didn't get remanded to their eighth-grade teacher's custody by the juvenile court judge unless they were in big trouble. They also knew that Miss Griffith would not raise her voice in anger or make them feel small and humiliated because of their mistake. She never did.

Charlie Rosenbaum and four of his eighth-grade classmates sat quietly and contritely in the modest front parlor of the Lipon Street house, waiting for the other shoe to drop. Miss Griffith concluded her exchange with the police and thanked them for escorting the boys to her home. Then she closed the door after the officers and turned her full attention to the young offenders.

She asked if they were all right and waited until each one had acknowledged her question with an affirmative nod. She asked if they were hungry, but legal action had a way of killing even growing boys' appetites.

Satisfied that immediate needs were met, Miss Griffith commenced with the day's lesson. Did they understand why the railroad detectives had turned them over to the authorities? Her question was met with shrugs and shaken heads, but the quickly downcast eyes told her the culprits were not as clueless as they hoped to seem.

Young Charlie burst out defensively that they frequently picked up coal around the tracks. He didn't know why they'd gotten all mad about it this time.

It was his teacher's turn to shake her head. She asked Charlie and his accomplices how this incident differed from their usual activity.

More than a question, it was an expectation. The ticking of the wall clock in the entryway grew uncomfortably loud as she awaited their response.

Finally, Jose Hernandez spoke up. In the past, they had merely picked up the pieces that fell off the coal cars. This time, however, he and some of the other boys had climbed up on a couple cars and actively encouraged some more pieces to fall out onto the ground.

Miss Griffith challenged them to think about how retrieving the coal was all right, but what they had done this time was not. As in the classroom at Twenty-fourth Street School, she encouraged them to figure things out for themselves, to think things through from all angles. Debates and self-expression were part of her curriculum. Thirteen- and fourteen-year olds were perfectly capable of tackling the issues of the day: Should the income tax amendment be adopted? Should women be able to vote in national as well as state elections?

Where is the line between scavenging and stealing?

Skillfully, she led the boys who had narrowly avoided jail to recognize the difference between unlawfully taking coal from railroad cars and lawfully picking it up outside the right-of-way after it had fallen from the cars and been abandoned by the company. On this occasion, and indeed at every opportunity, Emily Griffith impressed upon her students how privileged they were to live in America and how important it was to honor that privilege by being law-abiding citizens.

Fifty-five years later, Judge Charles Rosenbaum watched as an unrepentant juvenile offender he had sentenced was led from the courtroom. "There but for the grace of Emily Griffith," he thought, recalling the coal-stealing incident of his own youth, "might have gone I."[1]

––––––

Model citizen Emily Griffith was unusually well acquainted with the Denver police and the judicial system. The association grew naturally out of concern for the welfare of her students. Central and Twenty-fourth Street schools were in rough neighborhoods. Temptation and desperation were everywhere. Phone calls came at all hours of the night from folks in trouble who needed her help, and Miss Griffith regularly showed up at the police station or courthouse to plead the case of one student or another.

Denver youth who ran afoul of the law were luckier than most. In 1902, Judge Ben Lindsey had succeeded in establishing one of the first juvenile courts in the land. Prior to that time, boys and young men who broke the law—any law—were locked up right along with hardened criminals, helpless prisoners in a veritable "school for crime."

In his eye-opening 1910 book *The Beast,* Lindsey shocked the country with his revelation of "the abominable pollutions that had been committed upon their little bodies" while in custody. The stories he exposed, literally out of the mouths of babes, brought grown men to tears and inspired sweeping reform of the criminal justice system for juveniles.

A bantam rooster of a man, the "Kid's Judge" fought tooth-and-nail to create a more compassionate and effective way of dealing with underaged offenders. Adult laws and the criminal justice system, Lindsey believed, fed on fear and lies. "I found that when a boy was brought before me, I could do nothing with him until I had taken the fear out of his heart; but once I had gotten rid of that fear, I found—to my amazement—that I could do anything with him."[2]

Lindsey's "contributory juvenile delinquency" laws opened the way for the prosecution of parents for neglecting their children, as well as of "divekeepers" and gamblers who targeted and seduced the young. He also improved child labor laws and their enforcement.

Under Lindsey's juvenile court system, young lawbreakers were sent to a detention school rather than jail, or were released on probation to responsible adults such as Miss Griffith. "Our work, we find," said Lindsey, "is to aid the civilizing forces—the home, the school, and the church—and to protect society by making the children good members of society instead of punishing them for being irresponsible ones."[3]

The judge once came across a policeman insisting on the arrest of a couple of boys accused of stealing bicycles. It suddenly dawned upon

Lindsey the difference between the criminal approach to the situation and the methods of his juvenile court. "Officer," he said to the policeman, "You are trying to save bicycles. I am trying to save boys."[4]

As was Emily Griffith's vision, Judge Lindsey's ideas were championed by Frances Wayne and the *Denver Post*. His innovation also became a model for reform, and people from all over the United States and abroad wrote to him and visited Denver, asking how they might go about establishing a juvenile court system of their own. When it came to correcting and guiding boys in trouble, Ben Lindsey and Emily Griffith were like-minded allies.

As a teacher, Emily had long been concerned for the child who drifted into trouble and spent time in the state home for dependent children or the Industrial School for Boys, only to be released back into the same environment that had led to his downfall initially. Some were runaways from abusive homes; some castaways from families too poor to care for them; some orphans. Too many of them lived on the streets and wandered into the pool halls and other dives, "associating with companions who lowered their standards of morality and led to dishonesty and crime."[5] It seemed a self-perpetuating, inescapable cycle that could lead only to tragedy.

Many Denver police officers attended Opportunity School themselves, taking various business and public relations courses. When they recognized a boy in trouble from the school, they took him to Miss Emily. She repeatedly opened her own home to such boys, providing, if only for a short time, a stable and caring sanctuary where they might feel valued and safe. It wasn't long before she recognized that the needs were too great and too numerous for her to handle alone. For years, a nearby hotel let her charge rooms for the boys entrusted to her care by the police. It wasn't enough.

In 1927, three years after she was named to the board of control for the State Industrial School for Boys in Golden, Griffith used her own funds to put a down payment on a neglected old mansion at Number 9 Pearl Street. With the help of an association of charitable and civic organizations, she established this address as "A Home for the

Boy Who Needs One." Though not nearly as inspiring and memorable as the motto for Opportunity, it did succinctly state the home's purpose.

She "wanted to see boys have the privilege and pleasure of becoming self-supporting young men and make the right contacts with business and industrial leaders so that they might take their place as worthwhile members of our social order."[6]

Emily's own nephew, Richard "Dick" Griffith, provided a case in point. In 1926, when his parents, Charles and Minnie, decided to move from Denver to McCloud, Oklahoma, where Minnie had relatives, sixteen-year-old Dick elected to stay behind. He quit school to support himself by working as a messenger for a local bank, a hazardous job in the days when the streets were home to gangsters, like those who robbed the Denver Mint in 1922. Dick rarely spoke of or to his parents after their move to Oklahoma. Instead, it was Aunt Emily who persuaded him a few years later to get his equivalency degree from Opportunity's alternative high school. It was Aunt Emily who gave him financial assistance and a teaching job at her school when he undertook engineering studies at the School of Mines in Golden. And it was Aunt Emily who fairly burst with pride when Dick became the first in the family to earn a college degree.[7]

Number 9 Pearl accepted boys from fourteen to eighteen, and occasionally younger siblings who didn't want to be separated from their older brothers. "Boys under 16 attend school and work part-time; older ones may do the same or hold full-time jobs. Every lad assists with chores about the house."[8] Each boy was expected to pay part of his keep and to save 10 percent of his earnings as soon as he became employed.

Occupancy was limited to no more than twelve boys at any given time, to provide a more homelike atmosphere. Initially, Emily and her sister Florence personally managed Number 9. Later, a superintendent and housemother assumed the onsite management, guided by the prominent Denver citizens who made up the officers and directors. A large photo of Emily hung in the living room, inscribed, "To my boys."

Although many community organizations under the umbrella of The Denver Foundation contributed money, furniture, coal, and clothing to the home, by far the lion's share was shouldered by the Denver Kiwanis Club. The Kiwanians had long held a special place in their collective hearts for Miss Emily. First acquainted with the crusading educator through her campaign for the Opportunity School, they elected her a full member in 1920. When the National Kiwanis organization notified the Denver club that they could not admit women, they reluctantly changed her status to honorary member.

Emily Griffith epitomized everything the Kiwanis Club stands for. The club's objectives were her objectives:

- To give primacy to the human and spiritual rather than the material values of life.
- To encourage the daily living of The Golden Rule in all human relationships.
- To develop...a more intelligent, aggressive, and serviceable citizenry
- To cooperate in maintaining that sound public opinion and high idealism which foster the increase of righteousness, justice, patriotism, and goodwill.[9]

The Home for Boys became the most important service project in the history of the Denver Kiwanis Club. In fact, former members Bill Wafer and Dr. C. Robert Stankes co-founded the home with Miss Griffith. Traditionally, the club bought each resident a suit of clothes. Individual members personally mentored the boys, taking them along to their places of business to gain insider perspective and to make contacts, "building character and serviceable citizenship."

"CHEATED out of a Home, an Education, and a Chance to Make Good," read the front cover of a 1931 pamphlet for the home, "But No. 9 Pearl Street is on the Job." It was never intended as a permanent refuge; rather, it was "an oasis in the desert" until a young man could make it on his own. In its first four years of operation,

Number 9 served "233 Needy, Appreciative, Potential Citizens." In 1930 alone, ninety-seven boys were received by the home and eighty-two discharged. The list of "Leading Firms of Denver and Colorado Which Have Given Our Boys a Chance to Make Good" named forty-two employers, including Western Auto Supply, McGavens Bread Company, Mountain States Telephone, the Denver Dry Goods Company, the Albany and Olin Hotels, and Coors Porcelain Company.

Emily didn't like to talk about herself, claiming she was not really that interesting. She did like to talk about her boys of Number 9 Pearl.

The Kiwanis love affair with Miss Emily was unabashed from the beginning. It was at a 1935 luncheon meeting, with her as the only female member and the guest of honor, that one of the members first dubbed her the "Sweetheart of the Kiwanis Club." Paul Essert, Kiwanian and second principal of Opportunity, explained that the phrase "expressed a lot of the things we really felt about her, for no guy is going to call a gal his sweetheart unless she represents about everything in the world that he thinks is good."[10]

Emily took it all in with gracious smiles, but when she finally got her chance to respond to their use of the affectionate term, she said with good-natured humor, "It's nice of you to think of me in that way. But you know, I am getting awfully tired of this wholesale business of being a *group* sweetheart. Whoever heard of a woman getting a thrill out of taking a walk in the moonlight with her sweetheart group?!"[11]

Kiwanis was not the only organization proud to count Emily Griffith among its ranks. Arthur Baldwin, a former president of Denver Kiwanis, sang her praises to his wife, a member of the P.E.O. Sisterhood, an organization dedicated to promoting educational opportunities for women since 1869. Griffith had first spoken to Colorado P.E.O. Chapter E in 1918 on "The Work of the Opportunity School." Mrs. Baldwin invited her back for another program in January 1921. The ladies were so impressed that her name was voted upon favorably for membership, and on May 17, 1921, she was initiated into the sisterhood.

In her article on "Interesting Personalities in P.E.O." for the December 1929 *P.E.O. Record*, Florence Wilson Haines lauded Emily as "originator of the idea and founder of the Opportunity School, which has gained nation-wide attention as an institution, offering an education or vocational training to those without the advantages of a high school background. Especially does it serve Denver's foreign-born population seeking instructions in the principles and ideals of our Government."

In 1925, a group of bankers created the Denver Foundation, Colorado's first charitable community foundation. Along with notable business leaders, they invited Griffith to serve on the board of trustees because of her unique understanding of the community. Emily helped to shape the new organization throughout the 1920s, building into it the same flexibility and generosity of spirit that enabled the Opportunity School to grow and change in response to future needs.

Little wonder Griffith was nominated for the 1924 Woodrow Wilson Award by Dr. George Norlin, president of the University of Colorado, and Colorado Governor William E. Sweet. The prestigious national honor was designated to recognize "an individual or group that has rendered meritorious service to democracy, public welfare, liberal thought, or peace through justice." Though letters by the hundreds in support of Griffith were sent to the award committee, the $25,000 prize was presented instead that year to Lord Robert Cecil of England.

Nonetheless, Emily Griffith, eighth-grade graduate, was awarded numerous other recognitions: an honorary pedagogy degree from Colorado State Teacher's College (now University of Northern Colorado) in 1911, an honorary master of education from Colorado University in 1927, and a 1942 honorary humanities diploma from Colorado Women's College. Though undoubtedly gratified by the recognition of her educational peers, Emily was not greatly impressed by academic credentials or the initials signifying higher educational accomplishment attached to one's name. "It's what a person can *do* that ought to matter," the ever-practical schoolmarm insisted.[12]

Emily was the daughter of a frontier missionary, and membership in the Presbyterian Church remained important to her throughout her life. She drew strength and took comfort from religious study and worship. She attended both Capitol Heights Presbyterian Church at Eleventh Avenue and Fillmore, where her father served as an elder for several years, and Denver's Central Presbyterian Church. Designed by Brown Palace Hotel architect Frank E. Edbrooke and built with native Colorado sandstone and Tiffany stained glass in 1892, Central Presbyterian remains an extraordinarily beautiful edifice at 18th and Sherman.

By 1933, Emily Griffith had spent nearly fifty years taking care of other people—her family, her sister Florence, her prairie schoolchildren, her inner-city Denver pupils and their families, her wayward Pearl Street boys. Her light had radiated ever outward, illuminating countless lives. A burning desire to make things better, the glow of gratitude from those she had rescued and empowered, the energizing associations with philanthropic and community welfare organizations, and the forge of her faith all continued to fuel her inner fire.

Opportunity was by this time an established, smooth-running success. Number 9 Pearl was in the capable hands of the Kiwanis Club. The time had come at last for Emily Griffith to take care of herself—with a little help from her friends.

9
Out of the Mainstream

*T*he term *burn-out* may not have existed in the 1930s, but the reality did. More than 100,000 Denver citizens had passed through the Opportunity School's doors and past the principal's hallway desk. After nearly half a century of selfless giving, of dedicated devotion to the dreams of others, and of personal involvement in the lives of her students and her "boys," Emily Griffith's well was running dry.

"Miss Emily Griffith Resigns as Head of Opportunity School" read the December 14, 1933, *Denver Post* headline. After seventeen years as principal, Miss Griffith was "too tired to continue in active duty." Despite the public perception that she was retiring early, she was, in fact, only a few months shy of age sixty-five. A temporary leave-of-absence had been insufficient. The newspaper reported that she "for the past year has been living in her Pinecliffe cabin [and] will continue there throughout the winter."

Syndicated columnist Ernie Pyle, who visited the internationally famous retired educator years later, understood her emotional and physical exhaustion. "Emily Griffith…bogged down under years of helping other people," he explained. "She got so other people's miseries were too much for her. She couldn't bear to look at sadness or hear of trouble. She was worn out. She had to resign. She came up to this cottage which she had been building. When she got here, she couldn't sit up longer than half an hour at a time."[1]

Emily had purchased a lot in Pinecliffe, Colorado, in 1928. The small mountain resort community was 40 miles from Denver, 17 miles southwest of Boulder, up Coal Creek Canyon. Her youngest sister and brother-in-law, Ethel and Evans Gurtner, owned property adjoining hers, though they did not live there year-round until Ethel herself retired from teaching at Opportunity in 1941.

Former Opportunity School instructor and skilled carpenter Fred W. Lundy was a dear friend of the Griffith sisters. Along with Evans Gurtner, he built Emily and Florence a primitive but comfortable pine slab cabin on south Boulder Creek as a retreat from the city. Fred later lived with the sisters while he constructed a similar creekside cabin for himself about a mile farther up the canyon.

Fred Lundy was solicitous and considerate of the elderly sisters. He chopped firewood, ran errands for them, performed various handy-man tasks around the house and property, and often shared meals with them.

Emily and her sister subsisted on a mere $50 a month, the standard pension granted Denver Public School teachers. DPS officials, conscious of Griffith's international status, offered her double the usual stipend, along with a paid position as consultant for the Opportunity School. Emily rejected both, offering this rationale: "The first one because what is to be done for me should be done for *all*; if $50 a month isn't enough for me, it isn't enough for any teacher. And the second because I don't believe much in those 'advisory' jobs."[2]

She maintained that DPS pensions were disgracefully low and should be increased. Likewise, she complained, teacher salaries should be upped to a minimum of $1,500 per year, "as demanded by teachers who recently marched upon Governor Vivian's office." An outspoken advocate for her colleagues in the classroom, Emily Griffith's aim was "to rise not *from* the ranks, but *with* them."[3]

Money and material possessions were never very important to Emily. Personal pride was what she valued, and her self-worth was always based on something more profound than worldly goods. "You don't have to admit to the world that you don't have things,"[4] she often told her nephew's wife, Lois, in her later years. Fine people, Griffith insisted, did not necessarily come from fine circumstances.

In March of the following year, at the suggestion of Superintendent of Schools A. L. Threlkeld, the name of the school—which now covered the entire block from 12th to 13th avenues along Welton Street—was officially changed to the Emily Griffith Opportunity School (EGOS). Ever modest, she resisted the honor initially, but was soon persuaded by friends and associates that it was merely right and proper. "It is like having a monument to yourself that you can see," she confessed happily.[5]

The Griffith sisters lived simply in the mountains, out of preference as much as economic necessity. Their primitive but homey cabin lacked indoor plumbing, electricity, and a telephone. Bookshelves lined the pine-paneled walls, filled with old favorites and inspirational periodicals, religious tracts and education texts. It must have reminded them of the Nebraska homestead of their youth. Life became a sort of "adventure in contentment."[6] They had left the pressures and clamor of Denver far behind, but their many close friends and associates found the way to their door.

Paul Essert, Emily's successor as principal of the Opportunity School, was a frequent visitor. He sought her advice, kept her apprised of developments, and enjoyed her company. He later recalled her favorite clearing along the creek bank where she loved to sit and enjoy the mountain sounds and scents for hours. If she were lonely, she assured him, she could easily summon neighbors to come for a chat by banging a stick on an empty coffee can, "like the old American tom-tom." Friends gathered for a bonfire or simply to talk and share experiences or ways to cope with the isolation of mountain life.

Essert kept Emily's vision on track throughout the Depression years. He relied on the support and assistance of Assistant Principal Mrs. Mary Fenton Miller, who had served in that capacity alongside Griffith since the school's inception. Three days after the announcement of Griffith's resignation had run in the newspapers, Colorado Governor Adams had suggested the school be closed as part of his general retrenchment policy, which cut funding to public schools across the state. Denverites rallied to the school's defense, demanding a reassessment of its value to the community. Opportunity was spared, but its teachers suffered drastic and demoralizing pay reductions.

Under Essert's leadership, the school established a department coordinator system to avoid duplication of class offerings. Programs were divided into Public Service Occupations, Trades and Industry, Distributive Occupations, and Civic and Social Education. In 1936, Opportunity's Advisory Committee plan was officially established. To alleviate some of the congestion at the main facility, EGOS Instructional Centers began to operate in shops and plants, churches, hospitals, civic buildings, and even homes throughout the city.

Emily spent her retirement years reading, enjoying nature, and answering fan mail from current and former students, teachers, and associates, as well as from strangers who had heard of her accomplishments and wished to emulate her. Letters like this one surely warmed her heart:

> Opportunity School is giving me a chance to pick up the loose ends of my incomplete education. To me, education means more than training. It means culture. It means broadening my outlook on life and a chance to be of greater service to others.
>
> Opportunity is a place where I can come in my clean cotton housedress and after I am here forget that I cannot dress as elaborately as some of my seemingly more fortunate fellow women.
>
> I feel like I have a chance all over again. I am gaining self-confidence, which will mean self-reliance. Possibly I may become a financial aid to a husband who has so diligently labored against physical handicaps left by the great and horrible world war.[7]

Tucked away in Manuscript File #1514 at the Colorado Historical Society are dozens of yellowed newspaper joke columns, which Emily had carefully clipped, week after week. "It's Legal to Laugh" was shamelessly corny, including such groaners as:

First man: "How long have you been working for Doodle &
Company?"
Second man: "Just since they threatened to fire me."

Mrs. Black: "I think that Smithers boy is just a bad egg."
Mrs. White: "Oh no, he's too fresh for that."

Surely Griffith would be tickled to know this collection is one of
her few personal items available to researchers today.

Ernie Pyle visited Emily's cabin in September 1936. "No matter in
what city this article is published," Pyle wrote, "somebody will read it
who knows Emily Griffith. For she is the mother, the soul, the spirit, the
everything of Opportunity School. There are a quarter-million people, I
expect, who know her and love her. I have seen a few like her before, but
very few indeed. She is one who really lives for other people."[8]

Denver School Superintendent Charles E. Green, his family, and
their young friend, Jeanne Varnell, called upon the sisters in 1937.
Varnell recalled that the women received them warmly: "The sisters
wore long, dark skirts and shirtwaists, possible holdovers from World
War I days...The four-room building—Spartan even for a summer
cabin—was the sisters' year-round residence. The interior was
scrubbed and tidy, yet it gave the visitors the eerie feeling of stepping
back into an earlier era."[9] Wood was stacked next to the cookstove, a
pitcher and basin served as the kitchen sink, and kerosene lamps awaited
the darkness. The guests sat around a rustic oilcloth-covered table and
enjoyed the simple refreshments served by Florence.

When the United States entered World War II, Opportunity mobilized under the War Production Board, operating a round-the-clock and
training 24,000 men and women for defense work. Now, in Pinecliffe
during these years, Miss Griffith began to receive another sort of visitor.
The railroad ran right through the center of town and near her cabin.
She remembered, "Soldiers on their way to the front or on the way home
stopped by and tell me they had been helped at Opportunity School."[10]
The former principal never tired of hearing their stories.

Opportunity's third principal, Graham Miller, took the reins during World War II. The school played a significant role in the federally funded National Defense Training Program. Additions to the facility in 1940–1941 included an airframe shop, new auto mechanics and machine shops, a foundry, and a heat treatment plant.

Every department of the school responded to wartime demands in its own way. Trades and Industry added metal casting and, incredibly, shipbuilding, using prefabricated parts from Mare Island Navy Yard. Many programs operated all day every day, and classes were offered for air-raid wardens, food conservation, and victory gardening. Enrollment in the school's high school classes dropped almost 50 percent during these years due to military enlistments, though at long last, Opportunity was allowed to award diplomas for the successful completion of its nonacademic programs.

After the war, returning armed services veterans enrolled by the hundreds, seeking skills that could translate into rewarding civilian employment. The Agriculture Department offered popular courses in fur farming and poultry raising. Insurance and real estate classes had long waiting lists. The new Family Life Education program filled an important need for countless couples poised to launch the postwar baby boom.

Tiny Pinecliffe had no church when Emily Griffith retired there, so she held Sunday gatherings at her cabin. Usually seven or eight people came, but there were sometimes as many as twenty, "which," she said, "is about all the living room can hold." Her guests were of all ages and denominations, as might be expected. Sometimes they would share a potluck supper or picnic lunch. Emily never presumed to teach Sunday school, though she often gave inspirational talks. "I just do the reading. We learn the Bible together. We find in it courage and hope." She often invited complete strangers, including railroad workers and transients, to join the group, and sometimes managed to obtain a little melodeon to accompany the hymns.[11]

Though Emily insisted she was quite comfortable in Pinecliffe, her Kiwanis Club friends were dismayed by her living situation and offered to modernize her cabin. Eventually, they installed electricity for heating, lighting, and cooking, as well as indoor plumbing—with the enthusiastic help of volunteers who were Opportunity graduates of the trades programs.

In a December 2, 1946, letter to the Denver Kiwanis Club, Emily implored the members, "Please let me be on good terms with myself and let me know the amount of the expenditures. The debt I owe for your expressed belief in me during the years at Opportunity can never be paid."

Jack Beatty responded on behalf of the club in a letter to her ten days later: "The costs of the improvements have all been taken care of by a few of your good friends. We were most happy to do this little bit for you…and we want you to accept it with our love, best wishes, and highest regards."[12]

Griffith visited Denver for special occasions such as the school's twenty-first birthday party in 1937. She was the guest of honor, presiding over 500 distinguished guests at a dinner in the stylish Denver Dry Goods tearoom. In 1939, she returned to the city to receive the Eminent Service Award from the Colorado Press Association. In 1945, she opened the annual Red Cross drive. The high-profile event was held in the Presidential Suite of the Brown Palace Hotel, and Emily was featured in the society columns—"the last place any one would expect to find me!"[13]

The tribute that most touched her heart was staged by her friends in the Denver Kiwanis Club on June 26, 1946. The tribute, titled "A Rose for Miss Emily," was held in the Cathedral Room of the Albany Hotel. Many honored guests attended the luncheon, including Mayor Benjamin Stapleton, School Superintendent Charles Greene, *Post* reporter Frances Wayne, one of the boys from No. 9 Pearl Street, and Howard Johnson, fourth principal of Opportunity.

Each speaker who took a turn at the microphone showered the guest of honor with compliments and praise and handed her three long-stemmed roses. She was called "sweetheart" and "darling." Letters, some of which were probably typed by Opportunity graduates, from invited guests unable to attend provide a sampling of what the tributes were like. Mary Lathrop, Denver's first female attorney, wrote Emily: "I always think of you in connection with what someone wrote of Thomas Jefferson. They spoke of his influence as 'the lengthening shadow of one man.'"

"You have a gift with which few are endowed," wrote Clem W. Collins of the First National Bank, "the faculty of inspiring people to improve themselves and thus to make better citizens. Many are those who will grasp the torch passed on by you and who will carry on the work in different ways…different, but I doubt if there is another individual to be found who could do the great works…in the humble manner in which you have achieved your constructive work."

Former neighbor Charles Ford Hansen recalled, "We owe a big debt of gratitude to you, Mom and I, for the offer of a teaching position at Opportunity School, a position Mom still holds and which made possible our home and my education."

"Were I ever called upon to choose the one person of my acquaintance whom I considered as having rendered the most unselfish and uplifting service toward the welfare of her fellow man," testified Frederick C. Emmerich of the U.S. Department of Immigration, "my decision would unhesitatingly be…Emily Griffith."

U.S. Senator and perennial Colorado politician "Big Ed" Johnson wrote from Washington, "The noble purpose of your quiet but forceful endeavor has about it that quality of greatness which is the handiwork of only a few…of a given generation. I cannot begin to estimate the number of men and women inspired by your courage, helped by your ingenuity, cheered by your never-failing spirit of service."[14]

By the end of the program, Emily Griffith's arms were filled with roses and her eyes were filled with tears. Overwhelmed, the petite, fragile educator sighed, "I feel two inches taller."[15]

The event had been limited to Kiwanians and their special invited guests, but when the newspapers ran an announcement of the private tribute, *Time* magazine sent its representatives over to the Kiwanis offices. An article on the school had been written and was waiting for something such as this tribute to "break it." Griffith had no idea these national reporters were in the audience and accepted everyone present as old friends whom she had not seen for a long time. Five cameras were flashing constantly, but it did not seem to bother her at all.

When at last the guest of honor was called upon, the lights went out and a spotlight from the ceiling shone down upon Miss Emily and the roses alone. When the lights came back up, they illuminated a standing ovation.

Emily gave one of her little talks—it could not be called a speech—relating the success stories of others. She spoke for around ten minutes about students who had overcome great obstacles and hardships, taking no credit for herself, and ended with a recital of the Twenty-third Psalm as given to her "by an Indian chieftain." Denver radio station KOA recorded the entire program and rebroadcast it that evening. Despite the poor quality of the sole surviving copy of the tape, one can still hear the sweetness, sincerity, and gentle humor in Emily Griffith's sometimes quavering voice. Apparent above all else is the warm way in which all present responded to her.

In concluding her remarks that memorable afternoon at the Albany Hotel, her close friend Frances Wayne commented, "Surely more of us should give our roses while eyes can see and ears can hear."[16]

Less than one year later, on June 17, 1947, upon receiving her annual card of honorary Kiwanis membership, Emily wrote club president Aksel Neilsen, "The thrill of receiving [the card] never grows old. It is my most prized possession, and brings many happy memories."[17]

Within twenty-four hours of penning the short but heartfelt note, Emily Griffith was gone.

10
Troubled Waters

The shocking news blared from radios and dominated headlines on Thursday evening, June 19, 1947.

FAMOUS EDUCATOR AND SISTER ARE FOUND SLAIN AT PINECLIFFE.

Slain—there was nothing ambiguous or subtle about it. Emily and Florence Griffith had each been shot in the back of the head and left lying in pools of blood. Reports stated that the bodies were discovered in their mountain cabin around 7:30 a.m. by Evans and Ethel Gurtner, sister and brother-in law of the victims. Boulder County sheriff's officers were immediately summoned to the scene.

The *Denver Post* ran a photo of Chips, the elderly sisters' cocker spaniel, scratching on the Griffith cabin door, captioned, "alone and bewildered in a suddenly strange world."[1] Most who heard the news felt much the same.

It wasn't right. A life lived so selflessly for others should not end this way. Alongside the front page accounts of the crime ran summaries of Emily Griffith's accomplishments and legacy. "She had the courage to stick to her dream until she made it a reality," Opportunity School principal Howard Johnson told the *Denver Post*. To the 20,000 persons enrolled in the school that year, the stunning loss of Miss Emily was personal.

The disbelief felt by so many was expressed in an emotional editorial in the *Rocky Mountain News* on June 20: "This could not be true.

She who had given nothing but kindness during her entire life, she who had lifted the lowly and offered them hope, she who had brought learning to those who otherwise would have walked in confusion, she who had refused the comforts of the world for the humble pleasure of instilling pride in others—she, they said, had been slain by an assassin's hand."

The *Denver Post* editor wrote that day with the same sense of appalled outrage about "The Passing of a Bold Spirit." "Behind an exterior which…seemed almost prim, [Emily Griffith] possessed a bold, restless spirit—bold enough to break with the traditional views of education…restless enough to try to do something about the shortcomings of the school system as she saw them."

Governor Robert Knous himself told reporters, "Colorado has lost one of its greatest citizens. She did as much as anyone in this country to bring civilization, culture, and enlightenment to the west. Words cannot express my grief."[2]

It made no sense. The elderly women had little money or property to speak of. As prominent Denver socialite Mrs. Claude Boettcher put it, "Miss Griffith was a kind and wonderful woman. It does not seem possible that such a philanthropist could have had an enemy."[3]

What possible motive could there be for the murders? The first hours of the investigation yielded not the slightest hint. Mystery surrounded the crime scene. All the windows and the door of the cabin had been locked. Food prepared for dinner was untouched. No signs of either a struggle or the murder weapon were in evidence. One slug was found in the bedstead near Florence's body. Boulder County sheriff's ballistics and identification officer Ed Tangen told reporters he had determined the bullets were from a .38 caliber, fired at close range from a Smith & Wesson or a Colt pistol. The sisters' ages were reported as sixty-six for Florence, sixty-seven for Emily, but in the unflattering front page "last pictures" published in the two major Denver papers, Emily Griffith looked every one of her actual seventy-nine years of age.

Coroner Norman Howe placed the time of death around 7:00 Wednesday night, June 18. He later revised his estimate to 4:00–4:30 p.m., based on the condition of the bodies and statements of neighbors who said the sisters generally ate their evening meal around that time.

Prior to the fatal incident, Florence Griffith was virtually unknown. As one newspaper item put it, the double murder "brought to light a strange and obscure fact in the life of the prominent woman [Emily]. Few people of Denver, even close associates of the widely known Miss Griffith, were aware she had a sister, Florence."[4]

The June 19 edition of the *Rocky Mountain News* advanced a possible motive for the slayings. "Neighbors and friends of the sisters and [Fred] Lundy pointed out that Florence Griffith in the past year had become an increasingly heavy burden in the life of Emily Griffith. She had been in ill health for many years and recently had shown signs of failing fast. Lundy, they said, on many occasions had expressed grief over the 'martyr' life which Emily had spent in caring for her sister. On occasion he expressed the sentiment that he would 'rather see them dead than the way they are living.'"

And then there was the car.

Locked and parked beside South Boulder Creek, Lundy's '41 Nash sedan was found the same day as the sisters' bodies, a half mile outside of Pinecliffe, about midway between the Griffith and Lundy cabins. Sheriff's officers, seeing a note inside against the windshield, broke a window and found a briefcase on the front seat. The case contained insurance policies, a deed, and neatly stacked small bills—all fives and tens—estimated to total about $350. The handwritten note was addressed simply to "Coroner."

> If and when I die, please ship body to Roscoe, Illinois, to be buried in our family plot. No autopsy. Correspond with Roy Cummings, Roscoe, Illinois (cousin). No funeral here. Masonic funeral there. Money in this briefcase can be used for immediate expenses. Thank you. P.S. Embalm at Boulder, Colorado.

It was signed "Fred Lundy."[5]

The Griffith sisters' nephew initially accepted the Boulder County investigators' conclusion. Dick Griffith, a petroleum engineer living in Lander, Wyoming, at the time, told the *News* that "Fred decided it would be best to kill my aunts because of advanced age and failing health."[6]

Thus was the mercy killing/suicide theory advanced. A nationwide search for Fred Wright Lundy was zealously undertaken. Quigg Newton, Denver's thirty-five-year-old mayor, ordered the cream of the Denver detective squad to assist in the investigation, using state-of-the-art crime lab gear. The detective sergeant spearheading the Denver probe had very personal reasons to pursue justice for the victim. Nearly half a century earlier, Charles J. Burns had been a student in Miss Griffith's sixth-grade class at Central School.

According to the *Boulder Daily Camera*, Lundy regularly shared meals with the sisters. He even had his own bed in their home. Emily and Florence occupied twin beds in the other bedroom.

Boulder County Undersheriff Don Moore told the *Denver Post* that Lundy "was known to be fond of Emily, but she did not reciprocate. [Her feelings were] more like a sister for a brother, or one old friend for another."[7] The source of this very personal information was never disclosed, but it seems likely to have been Ethel and Evans Gurtner.

Newly elected Mayor Newton decreed that all flags be lowered to half-mast to honor the slain educator. This despite the fact that her photo and appeal to Opportunity School alumni had been featured in newspaper advertisements urging them to support former mayor Ben Stapleton in the race against Newton only a month before.

Newton himself was unacquainted with Griffith, but his wife, Virginia, held the late educator in high regard. Her grandmother, former Colorado First Lady Virginia Shafroth, had attended Opportunity School in its earliest years to learn typewriting.[8] Denver papers quoted Mayor Newton as saying, "Her work, her faith in the power of education, her belief in humanity, will always endure as a magnificent example of American democracy."[9]

Both the *News* and the *Post* lived up to their sensationalist reputations by running murder scene photos, showing officers examining blood stains on the cabin floor, the uneaten dinner for three, Lundy's abandoned auto, the railroad water tank searched for Lundy's body, and various Pinecliffe residents interviewed by investigators. The *Post* even included a hand-drawn map of Pinecliffe by staff sketch artist Angelo O'Doristo showing the relative locations of the Lundy, Griffith, and Gurtner cottages, as well as the railroad, post office, and place where Lundy's car was found.

Frances Wayne, who described herself as Emily Griffith's "oldest, dearest, and most loving of friends," set down her memories in a June 20 piece for the rival *Rocky Mountain News.* The flowery eulogy illustrated the lack of journalistic objectivity for which she had been fired from the *Post,* less than a year earlier. It began, "Emily Griffith is dead! Oh no, she isn't, nor ever will be."

Wayne retold the story of how the two met during the 1915 Christmas charity drive, when the teacher first shared her idea for the Opportunity School. The reporter spoke of their "long, close, cherished friendship, kept aglow through the years by a profound reverence for her character, ideals, and simplicity." Going so far as to label Griffith "a Christ-like woman," Wayne cited "those qualities of heart and soul which made a certain Man of Galilee the object of veneration to his companions and of the ages." In closing, she commanded Emily to "take the place you have earned…because you had reached as near perfection as a human being may go."[10]

Shockwaves generated by Emily Griffith's murder were felt far beyond Colorado. She had become an internationally known figure, and her influence was more far-reaching than she would have imagined. A story wired in by the *Denver Post*'s Washington, D.C., correspondent, Phil J. Rodgers, a week after the murders dramatically illustrated Griffith's widespread impact.

Washingtonians, Rodgers reported, were abuzz and aghast at news of the crime. An elevator operator in the Senate building overheard two western senators discussing the murder and asked them for details. The man had never been west of the Potomac himself, but he "felt he knew Miss Griffith because she had done so much to help his younger brother who had gone to Denver many years ago for his health."[11]

Rodgers characterized the broader reaction in the nation's capital as puzzlement over why the renowned educator had been living in such dangerous isolation in a small mountain cabin. Was her retirement income so meager that she could not afford a house someplace more secure? Many felt that a home within the protected and patrolled limits of a city might have saved her life.

In fact, her sister Ethel revealed to the *Boulder Daily Camera* that Emily had retained ownership of her home in Denver until less than a year before her death. She resided permanently at the Pinecliffe cabin entirely by choice. She must have sensed that had she remained surrounded by the many needy people and desperate situations in Denver—and unable to attend to them all—she would have been overwhelmed. Florence, too, was probably much happier and at ease away from the clamor and complexities of city life.

Emily Griffith's obituary, titled "Murder in Pinecliffe," shared the "Crime" page of the June 30, 1947, issue of *Time* magazine with the "Murder in Beverly Hills" account of the '20s gangland-style "cut down" of notorious mobster Benjamin "Bugsy" Siegel, "a hood with class." Griffith, conversely, was characterized as "a kind of schoolmarm saint," revered by all Denver.

As the murder investigation and manhunt for Lundy proceeded at its own pace, final arrangements for Emily and Florence were made by their surviving sister, Ethel. A spokesman for Olinger Mortuary said that because of the condition of the bodies, the coffins would be unopened. The double funeral was scheduled for 2:30 in the afternoon, Saturday, June 21, in the Central Presbyterian Church of Denver, 1660 Sherman Street, which the sisters had attended for many years. Interim pastor Dr. Joseph Vance conducted the memorial service.

According to the *Denver Post*, "a kindly rain kept from the church morbid curiosity seekers."[12] A few hundred sincere admirers were not to be deterred. All three of the Opportunity School principals who had succeeded Miss Emily were present. Also among the mourners were true friends and people whose lives had been touched in one way or another by the school. Past and present students and staff came to pay their last respects to the compassionate and visionary woman who reimagined what public education could and should be and changed the face of education in America.

Mrs. Jessie Ford Hansen was an Opportunity student in the spring of 1918 when Miss Griffith went around to all the classes at term's end, saying she'd like to offer summer classes for which there were no funds and so was seeking volunteers to teach. Hansen had stepped up to the challenge, along with twenty others. She taught beginning shorthand all summer for nothing. At summer's end, Emily persuaded the school board to pay the volunteers for their lunches and carfare and managed to get each of them $50. Hansen had taught at the school continuously since.

Another veteran faculty member, Jerry N. Tobin, recalled the post–World War I incidence of a desperate and destitute student who considered suicide when he couldn't afford food for his family. Not only did Miss Emily buy groceries, coal, and milk for the family, and pay an insurance premium due the next day, but upon learning that the wife's father was a wealthy man, she even effected a reconciliation between the student and his father-in-law.

Though neither a student nor a faculty member, Frederick C. Emmerich remembered fondly his association with the school and its founder. In his official capacity with the federal Immigration and Naturalization Service, Emmerich had first become acquainted with Miss Griffith thirty-two years earlier when he visited the night school to examine candidates for citizenship. "I thought she was the most wonderful woman I had ever met," he told a *News* staff writer the day of the funeral, "and knowing her over the years has only strengthen (sic) that impression."[13]

Emily and Florence's nephew, Dick, who had always been close to his aunts, sat silently in a front pew with his wife, Lois, and three-year-old son, Russell. Newspaper accounts mention younger sister Ethelyn's presence, but apparently Evans did not accompany her to the service.

Also in attendance, but laying low, were detectives on the lookout for Lundy, should he appear at the service. Although they were aided by acquaintances of the former caretaker, no sightings were reported.

The Olinger "Funeral Book" listed 1880 as the date of birth for Emily, 1881 for Florence. The book described thirty-eight floral arrangements from the Denver Chamber of Commerce, the Business and Professional Women of Denver, the State Board of Vocational Education, the Colorado Education Association, the faculty of Opportunity School, and many others.

Six Kiwanians and six Denver Public School board members served as pallbearers. Two matching pink caskets were placed in front of the altar. A male quartet sang "Abide with Me," and the Twenty-third Psalm was read. As heavy rain continued to fall outside the church, Dr. Vance spoke of "mingled shadows and sunshine" symbolizing the occasion.[14]

Arthur Baldwin, accountant and past president of the Denver Kiwanians, delivered the eulogy. Emily Griffith, he said, "dipped her pen in life."

"Her heart," Baldwin intoned, "as big as humanity; her generous, creative spirit quickened the soul of Denver to high achievements. Because of its power to inspire, we keep the memory of what she has done vivid. Because the way she provided is now so clearly essential, we walk in it with increasing purpose."[15]

Following the benediction, the first to file past the caskets were young men from Number 9 Pearl Street, the home for wayward boys founded by Miss Griffith. At the close of the service, as the twin caskets were carried gently down the steps from the church to the hearses, biographer Elinor Bluemel claims that the clouds parted and a rainbow appeared. Newspaper accounts, however, do not confirm her affirmative finale and describe instead bared heads bowed in the hard rain. Older members of Central Presbyterian recalled that a piece of slate tile slid off the church roof and shattered on the pavement.[16]

A private cremation followed the memorial. The ashes of Emily and Florence Griffith were interred together in Denver's venerable Fairmount Cemetery. Their headstone bears no dates of birth.

11
Murky Depths

It was the sort of day twenty-year-old World War II veteran Jim Oakes had day-dreamed about throughout his Pacific tour of duty. He and friend Charlie Steinshouer, also a recently discharged Navy veteran, stood up to their waders in South Boulder Creek, enjoying the beautiful late summer weather. So what if they weren't catching anything with live bait and casting rods? The sun shone, the mountain air smelled of warm pine, and the stream rushed over stones with a sound like laughter.

Presently, Jim decided to head for a large boulder on the other side of the stream to see if his luck might improve. He gazed idly about his midstream throne and spotted something whiteish wedged beneath the overhang of a nearby rock. Was it a dead animal? He poked at it with the end of his rod, attempting to dislodge it.

Moments later, Jim stared in astonishment as a leg rose up from the water. The tip of his fishing pole had run through a shredded trouser leg. The bloated object had been human.

He yelled to Charlie. After venturing out to verify his friend's gruesome discovery, Charlie knew they'd have to find assistance and notify authorities.

Jim volunteered to stay with the body so as not to lose track of where it was. Charlie hesitated to leave his friend alone with the still submerged corpse, pointing out that it probably wasn't going anywhere. Jim assured him he'd be okay, but made him promise not to be gone long.

As his friend sped off, Jim settled in for the wait. Bodies didn't show up in Colorado mountain streams every day, and the mystery was irresistible. Who had this person been? Were there family, friends who cared and worried at the disappearance? What had transpired to bring about such a terrible end?

After some time, Jim got the idea to mark the beacon boulder with a big masking tape "X" so that it could still be found if Charlie didn't come back and he had to leave.

Charlie did come back—with a recovery team of nearly twenty men. They used grappling hooks and tied ropes around the body to drag it to the bank. As they wrestled with the decomposing mass of flesh, Oakes fought back an urge to retch.

Getting the remains up the steep, rocky slope above the stream to the railroad tracks was a struggle. The corpse was shoved into a rubber bag, then put on a railroad pumper handcar and taken to Pinecliffe nearby.

In the commotion surrounding the arrival of the body, residents crowded around the young man who had made the discovery. Still sickened and disturbed by the find, Jim was unprepared for the hero's welcome and outpouring of gratitude that enveloped him. Appreciative strangers expressed their relief that the man had been found, confessing to two months' anxiety, fearful he was lurking somewhere, ready to kill again. Their ordeal was finally over.

No word of compassion was spoken; not a tear shed. The dead man's culpability was as instantly assumed as was his identity. Jubilant locals invited the young men to breakfast next morning, patted them on the back, and even offered them fishing tips. But at the Steinshouer cabin that night, and on many nights thereafter, Jim Oakes had trouble sleeping.[1]

———

Even before the Griffith sisters were laid to rest, the manhunt for Fred W. Lundy was on. All agreed that his abandoned sedan with its stash of cash and instructions for the coroner was incriminating. Law enforcement officers forced their way into Lundy's locked cabin. Dirty dishes in the sink and a neatly made bed were discovered, but Undersheriff Moore reported they "found no further clues or information of significance."[2]

One day after the discovery of the murder victims, the *Boulder Daily Camera* dutifully reported Boulder County Sheriff Arthur Everson's tips for spotting the chief—and, in fact, only— suspect in the Griffith sisters' murders:

> Lundy likes good steaks. He eats in the better restaurants and stays in good hotels. He dresses fastidiously. Lundy smokes Camel cigarets (sic) heavily. He appears drawn and ill and is stooped.[3]

Lundy was described as sixty-one years old, five-feet-six inches tall, 150 pounds, of slight build, with brown eyes and thinning iron-gray hair. He was said to have very bowed shoulders and was reported to have been wearing glasses and a gray suit when last seen.

Old friend Walter Patterson, who had worked with Lundy years earlier at the Leyner Engineering Works, described him as "a quiet sort of fellow, but a good man. He had a well-used Bible and he loved the mountains." Patterson recalled Fred as a "swell dresser" who didn't drink or date in the years they boarded together. "Fred never said much about his family," Patterson told the *Rocky Mountain News,* "but he made a few trips back to Chicago to visit his father, who operated a meat market." He recalled that Lundy spent most of his weekend free time in the mountains during those years (1911-1914), taking the Saturday train and staying alone in a rented cabin until catching the last train back on Sunday.[4]

The day of the Griffiths' double funeral, law enforcement officers from Boulder and Denver met for three hours. When the conference concluded, they were still at a loss for a motive. Surely the slayer could only be a "madman."[5]

Dock Myron Teegarden, a ten-year veteran of the Boulder County Sheriff's Office who worked on the case, recalled, "There was a lot of guessing going on—there always is—as to possible reasons and suspects. But our consensus was there was really no mystery about it. He [Lundy] was going with Emily and she rebuffed him. And he always felt her sister was a problem."[6]

Deputy Coroner Norman Howe impanelled a six-man coroner's jury in preparation for a possible inquest, though he didn't expect to need them "unless there are further developments."[7] Undersheriff Donald Moore gave equal weight to three possibilities: Lundy shot himself, Lundy drowned himself, or Lundy hopped a freight and was still at large.

The search for Lundy's body, on the presumption that he had committed suicide, turned from the swollen waters of South Boulder Creek to the surrounding Roosevelt National Forest and back again. Grappling hooks were employed to probe a gravel pit pool as well as the turbulent creek. Hungry reporters pounced on every misstep. What might have been a body turned out to be an inner tube; a presumed man's shirt proved instead to be a dishtowel. Moore insisted that a shoe discovered in the creek had no possible connection with Lundy, denouncing media attempts to link the two as "malarkey."[8]

"The *Denver Post* especially leeched on to the story," Teegarden remembered. "They had two or three people focused on the case who accompanied the search party along the creek—all the way down to the impenetrable areas."[9]

Investigators studied Pinecliffe residents' statements connecting Lundy with the deceased. He was known by all to be a devoted friend of the Griffith sisters, spending more time at their cabin than at his own. His general demeanor in recent weeks, however, had struck many acquaintances as odd. Previously characterized as kindly, Lundy had been heard to remark, "Old people aren't any good to anybody; they shouldn't be allowed to live," and "When people get this old they ought to be shot."[10]

Seventeen-year-old Jim Morton was presumed to be the last to see the sisters alive. Around 3:30 p.m. on the 18th, he had delivered groceries to their cabin from Eklund's store. Lundy was there with the two women, he told detectives, and all three "seemed in good spirits."[11]

The grocer's wife, Mrs. Zara Eklund, reported a cryptic phone call received at the store around 3:00 p.m. the next afternoon, mere hours after the murders were discovered. A woman's voice asked if Fred Lundy was there. When Mrs. Eklund replied that he was not and asked to take a message, the caller replied, "No—no message," and abruptly hung up.[12]

Another Pinecliffe storekeeper, O. C. "Pop" Zerbst, told sheriff's department officials that Lundy "displayed peculiarities in his financial transactions," stating that Lundy often paid for the elderly sisters' groceries with new bills and asked for change in either new bills or silver. As if all this weren't suspicious enough, Zerbst confided to Boulder County sheriff's officers and reporters that "although Lundy did not care to hunt or fish, he frequently went away in the hills for several days, only to return in a cheerful mood."[13]

Zerbst saw Lundy driving his car a few minutes before 4:00 p.m. on Wednesday, June 18, the estimated time of the murders. According to Zerbst, the suspect was wearing a straw hat at the time. Soon thereafter, he noticed Lundy's car parked a short distance from the Griffith cabin.

Mrs. Alva Jamison, another Pinecliffe resident, reported seeing Lundy's car pulling out of his driveway around 4:00 p.m. Wednesday. She and her husband claimed to have heard a shot that evening at about 8:00, although no other residents said they did.

Elmo "Frosty" Peterson, a former University of Colorado basketball player of some repute, told detectives he had seen Lundy at approximately 8:00 p.m. on June 18, standing by the flooded gravel pit near the spot where his locked sedan was later found.

One of Pinecliffe's many summer residents, Dr. R. O. Buck of Cleveland, Ohio, claimed that, although he was unacquainted with Lundy, he had seen a man fitting his description at approximately 4:00 p.m. on June 18, leaving an automobile about two miles west of Pinecliffe. The man hopped over a barbed wire fence, Buck said, and leapt onto a freight near the trestle that spanned the creek. Pursuant to this lead, law enforcement officials asked police in Los Angeles, San

Francisco, and Salt Lake City to spread the alert, even as they continued to broadcast a pickup call for Lundy across the state and as far east as Illinois, where he had relatives.

Grand Junction police wired on June 26 that they were holding a man who strongly resembled Fred Lundy. A local doctor had alerted them to the suspicious character who had come to him for treatment of a leg wound. The injury, which the stranger claimed was the result of a black widow spider bite, turned out to have been inflicted instead by a .22 caliber bullet. Further investigation, however, identified the man as James R. Piper of Victorville, California. He was released, apparently on the assumption that if he were not Lundy, he could not be guilty.

Railroad officials, eager to cooperate, put their own detectives on the lookout for Lundy, shaking down railcars and "hobo jungles" for anyone matching his description. The railroad not only drained the large water tank near the spot where Lundy's car had been found, but also tore up some of the wooden supports beneath Pinecliffe's railroad trestle in order to dislodge trapped debris. Though no body was retrieved as the result of this effort, a man's straw hat was.

Sheriff Arthur Everson was in Pasadena, California, on vacation when news of the murders hit the papers. He telephoned Undersheriff Moore that Thursday evening to say he'd be leaving for home the next day.

On June 26, Moore disclosed to the press a new and disturbing piece of evidence brought to light by Fred's own brother, Jay M. Lundy of Hollywood, California. At the time, Jay was in Chicago visiting cousin Roy Cummings—the very cousin named in Fred's "suicide" note. Jay sent instructions via telegraph that a letter he'd recently received from Fred be turned over to the Los Angeles Police Department. W. J. Bradley, director of LAPD's detective bureau, quoted the letter as follows:

> If and when you should inherit one half of what I have, please give it all to Miranda {Fred's niece} when she is of college age. She will be fifteen the thirteenth of next January.

Don't come here. Wire Jim Lewis, attorney, Boulder, Colo.
He will take care of everything for you.

Nothing serious. Just wanted to get this off my mind.[14]

Although the letter was dated June 19, the postmark indicated it had
been mailed at the Pinecliffe post office on June 18, at 2:00 p.m.—two
hours before the Griffith sisters' estimated time of death.

What sort of inheritance was Lundy referring to? The self-
described handyman and inventor had retired from teaching at the
Opportunity School almost twenty years earlier. As far as anyone
knew, he had worked at odd jobs since. Yet Everson, upon looking into
the suspect's personal assets, discovered that in addition to his small
cabin and 40 acres of property, Lundy had $1,744 in the Colorado
National Bank in Denver, $1,000 in an Arvada bank, and $3300 in
cash, in addition to the money found in his abandoned automobile.
The funds totaled more than $6,000—a tidy sum for a retired carpen-
try instructor to stash away in the 1940s. The sheriff investigated a
report that Lundy had inherited a substantial amount of money upon
his mother's recent death, but it was, in fact, a small sum, sufficient
only to pay her bills and burial expenses.

What, then, was the source of his income? By most measures,
Fred Lundy lived modestly. A July 17 story in the *Denver Post*
disclosed Moore's discovery, "after a long and tedious check of
Boulder county courthouse records," that the suspect owned a 20-
acre placer mining claim in a remote part of the mountains above
Pinecliffe.[15] Might this essentially secret property have netted Lundy
a return over the years?

The *Camera* ran a bizarre story June 26, under the headline,
"Skeleton of Leg Found on Deputy Sheriff's Car With Note." Deputy
Sheriff Teegarden had discovered the complete skeleton of an actual
human leg and foot adorning the spotlight of his automobile outside
the courthouse that morning. Wrapped around the wired–together
bones was a handwritten note asking "Is this Fred Lundy?" According

to the report, "The skeleton later was hung on the sheriff's office door, much to the disturbance of Mrs. Neva Williams, the office deputy."[16]

Emily Griffith's will was filed in Boulder County court on June 28. Sole surviving sister Ethel Gurtner was designated executrix of the estate by Judge William E. Buck. The estate consisted of a bank account totaling about $9,500, a surprisingly large amount, considering Emily's meager retirement income. Most of the savings probably came from the sale of her Denver house less than a year before. In addition, the Pinecliffe property was estimated to be worth about $2,500. Pending the customary notice to creditors, calling for any claims against the estate, the $12,000 inheritance could not be distributed until six months had elapsed.

Dick Griffith recalled Aunt Emily mentioning several personal items she wanted him to have when she passed away, including family photographs, old newspaper clippings, and the watch given her by the Denver Kiwanis Club. He never got them. Years later, he recalled bitterly how the Gurtners swooped up everything of value immediately after the murders, including the mementos intended for him.

The will was dated December 6, 1946, and witnessed by Emily's attorney, State Senator Claude W. Blake, and Denver police judge Hubert B. Haney. Her entire estate was bequeathed to "my beloved sister, Florence." Ethelyn Griffith Gurtner was named contingent heir, "should said beloved sister [Florence] pre-decease me."[17]

Florence left no will. The stipulation in Emily's will that her estate went to Ethel only if Florence died before their eldest sister raised a difficult question. Because both were murdered on the same evening, did Florence, in fact, pre-decease Emily? If she did not, what were the implications for Ethelyn's entitlement?

Officer Ed Tangen rendered the brief controversy moot by declaring there was no way to know which of the Griffith sisters had expired first. He concluded that only a few seconds had elapsed between the deaths. Ethel Gurtner's claim to her sister's property was contested no further.

Tangen was a self-taught ballistics and identification expert. An accomplished commercial photographer by trade, the anti-social man had turned to documenting crime scenes sometime during the Depression. Tangen dabbled in fingerprinting and ballistics with equipment he designed himself. "His laboratory work and photomicrographs convicted many felons, set precedents in the courts, found their way into national publications, and earned acknowledgement of the FBI."[18]

Tangen had suffered a stroke in May 1943, which had left his left hand and arm partially paralyzed. Everson kept him on the force out of compassion, and Tangen was still on the job at age seventy-four when he entered the Griffith murder case.

Though he initially declared that the bullets that killed the sisters were fired from a .38 caliber Smith & Wesson or a Colt pistol, Tangen abruptly backpedaled when it was learned that Lundy was not known to possess a Smith & Wesson. "Tangen emphasized that [it] was fired either from a Harrington & Richardson or a Hopkins & Allen."[19]

On July 1, the *Boulder Daily Camera* declared in a headline, "Brother Hopes Fred Lundy Will Be Found Dead—Says He and Other Relatives Have No Knowledge of Suspect's Whereabouts." In a letter from Chicago, Jay Lundy told Sheriff Everson that he was "sure none of the relatives will try to cover him if he appears." Jay further stated that the cousin with whom he was staying—the Roy Cummings named in Fred's note—"knows no more than I." Though rumors circulated that Jay Lundy intended to oversee his brother's property, his letter to Everson stated that he was headed to Ohio, not Colorado, upon concluding his visit to Illinois.

Reportedly, Fred had been planning a trip to Chicago right before he disappeared. He had asked Emily to accompany him.

Deputy Coroner Howe continued to hold the cash found on the front seat of Lundy's sedan. A hasty count when the briefcase was first discovered put the total at $350. A later recount of the small bills revised that total to $555.

On July 3, an anonymous Denver man offered a $100 reward for Lundy's capture, dead or alive, were he to be found by anyone other than Boulder County sheriff's officers. In response, Everson was quick to declare that he was "not authorizing any organized groups to search for Lundy." He warned, "There is still a chance that Lundy is still alive, and the sheriff's office is not sure that he would allow himself to be taken without a struggle. Since he has already killed two persons, he might try to kill others who attempted to take him."[20]

The atmosphere in Pinecliffe was dampened by the tragedy and by days of heavy rains. The waters of swollen South Boulder Creek ran high. In the rock-strewn roiling stream, a body would be difficult to spot. On July 10, the flow of South Boulder Creek was cut to aid the search for Lundy's body. Denver water rights engineer H. L. Potts offered to divert Fraser River water reaching the creek via the Moffat Tunnel. Sheriff Everson eagerly accepted.

Everson arranged for nine Lowry Field army volunteers, trained in criminal investigation and led by Major Donald Young, to assist Teegarden. They dragged the creek from the point where Lundy's car had been found to the dam above Eldorado Springs, a distance of eight to ten miles. The first day's search proved fruitless.

The stretch covered on the second day included choppy rapids and falls. The Denver Water Commission now announced it would drain the reservoir above Eldorado Springs, a routine practice scheduled periodically to clean out accumulated sand. This time, however, officials kept close watch for a body, though few believed it would travel that far downstream from Pinecliffe.

Meanwhile, a man matching Lundy's description was reportedly seen in Durango, more than 300 miles to the southwest. A hotel proprietor there informed La Plata County Sheriff Chester Petty that the suspicious man had tried to rent a room. Sheriff Everson, however, dismissed the report out-of-hand, telling reporters it was merely "another of many rumors which have come from many parts of the state."[21]

On the third day, a piece of flesh found in the murky creek waters by the Lowry soldiers seemed to signal the party's first break. The malodorous specimen, about an inch thick and three inches square, was found four or five feet from the creek bank. Investigators immediately dispatched it to University of Colorado labs for tests by

Charles R. Bitter, professor of biology. A few days later, when the professor determined that the organic material was neither human flesh nor beef flesh (the full extent of the lab's analytical capability), the search of the creek was abandoned.

After two days' rest, the Lowry team began searching on land for Lundy. This time, the soldiers were accompanied by Undersheriff Moore, who wanted to focus the search on the mountainsides around Pinecliffe. He and other authorities now believed that Lundy's body might be hidden by thick underbrush. Lundy might even still be alive and hiding out in one of many deserted mine shacks or vacant cabins. This new phase of the dragnet was expected to take at least a week. It was July 17.

Apprehension among residents grew. Many summer residents cut short or forsook their usual Pinecliffe sojourn. Imaginations galloped unreined. Could there be a murderous maniac lurking nearby, his sites set upon other unsuspecting innocents? Mrs. Alma Gilcher's cabin had been violated the Sunday following the murders. The intruder had gained entrance to her summer home by breaking a window. Papers and drawers had been ransacked. No food or firewood was taken.

Ironically, Lundy himself had recently petitioned the Boulder County Sheriff's Office for a commission as a special deputy sheriff, citing an organized gang of thieves in the Pinecliffe area. Sheriff Everson had received no reports of theft in the area at that time and refused Lundy's request.

As the sweltering summer wore on, interest in the Lundy manhunt subsided. With no new developments and without fanfare, the Lowry soldiers, the sheriff's officers, and the Denver police stopped looking for the retired teacher or his remains. By the end of July, they conceded there was little likelihood that any identifiable remains would ever be found.

Two weeks later, that assumption proved premature when Jim Oakes and his friend went fishing in South Boulder Creek. The young Navy veteran's gruesome discovery appeared to close the case.

Fred Lundy's corpse, surprisingly well-preserved by the icy waters, was identified by Dr. S. F. Brennan, the Denver dentist who had made

Lundy's partial denture. According to the *Denver Post*, the body was further identified by a "slightly deformed right thumb."[22] The body showed no signs of bullet wounds or any evidence of violence. Neither inquest nor autopsy was undertaken, although autopsies were generally standard in cases where cause of death was unknown. Three days after he was dragged from South Boulder Creek, Lundy's body was cremated on the order of his brother, Jay.

Back home in Lakewood, Jim Oakes and Charlie Steinshouer basked somewhat uneasily in their fifteen minutes of fame. Everyone had heard about their discovery on the radio. The young men were delighted to split the $100 reward for finding the body.

Curiously, the ballistics report from the murders was changed at about this same time. Ed Tangen had originally declared the sisters were shot with a .38 caliber weapon. Officials now claimed that they had been slain with a .25 caliber weapon—the type of gun Lundy was known to have possessed.

Sheriff Everson and Coroner Howe pronounced the crime a murder/suicide and declared the case officially closed. The mystery, however, was still far from solved. No murder weapon—neither .38 nor .25 caliber—was ever found. No eyewitness ever came forward. And Fred Wright Lundy's side of the story would never be known.

Questions remain to this day. Why did a boy deliver groceries to the sisters' cabin that afternoon when Lundy, who regularly performed such errands, had just driven past the store on his way to the Griffiths' place? Why would a gentle man who rarely hunted use a gun to end the sisters' lives? Why would a mercy killer choose such a ruthless method, rather than poison or some other indirect or compassionate means? Why would he execute them right before they all sat down to dinner, rather than waiting until they were asleep? How could a friend who obviously cared deeply for the women have left them in such a callous manner, facedown in their own blood?

Who stood to benefit from the deaths? Crime investigators and murder mystery buffs know this is the fundamental question to consider. The Griffith sisters may not have had much in the way of worldly goods, but with both gone, Ethelyn and her husband, Evans, got it all. For years, Evans Gurtner had had periodic financial difficulties. At the time of her death, Emily Griffith had more money than she had ever had in her life, deposited following the January 1947 sale of her Denver home.

Evans was rumored to have connections to organized crime.[23] While he had a solid alibi at the time of the slayings, having spent the day in Denver with Ethel, could he have arranged for a third-party "hit" on the elderly sisters, knowing that their modest—but not negligible—savings and property would revert to his wife? The execution-style slayings seem to support such speculation.

Pinecliffe summer residents Robert and Laura Blake, interviewed by the *Denver Post* upon the fiftieth anniversary of the Griffith slayings, expressed serious doubts regarding Fred Lundy's involvement in the case. Then in their nineties, the Blakes were personally acquainted with Lundy and insisted, "We just knew he wasn't that kind of man." The fact that no autopsy was performed on Lundy's body struck the Blakes as particularly suspicious. "We are very sure he did not do it," they told the reporter.[24]

Biographer Yale Huffman recalled interviewing another longtime Pinecliffe resident in the late 1980s. He reported that when he asked her about Emily's murder, "she looked me straight in the eye and said, 'That brother-in-law of hers—he done it. I know he done it.'"[25]

And what of Fred Lundy? In light of the letter he wrote to his brother immediately before the slayings and the so-called suicide note left in his car, there can be no question that he knew a matter of life and death was imminent. In the weeks prior to the crime, Lundy reportedly talked often about old age. Might the sixty-two-year-old's romantic illusions with regards to Emily have been shattered by the revelation that she was not merely a few years his senior, as he'd long assumed, but was, in fact, closer to twenty years older than he?

Lundy's anguish over the sisters' deteriorating health and the increasing burden Florence presented for Emily was undoubtedly genuine. Perhaps Evans managed to convince him that putting the women out of their misery was the merciful thing to do. He might have told Fred he knew someone who could take care of it and that it would be best for everyone.

Fred may have even bought into such a plan, without any idea of when and how the deed would be done. Perhaps, like Judas, he found he could not live with himself when confronted with the horrendous outcome of what he'd helped to put into motion. Or perhaps, as an inadvertent witness to the crime, Lundy was compelled to take his own life or was drowned by the killer himself.

Early in the investigation, some of the Denver police officers suggested that part of the note found in Lundy's abandoned car appeared to have been written by someone else. Officer Tangen, whose self-taught forensic skills included handwriting analysis, flatly decreed that the instructions to the coroner were all written by the same person and that the handwriting corresponded with papers found in Fred's cabin.[26]

The truth in all these matters may never be known.

A review of the Boulder County Sheriff's Office records of the investigation could be of great help in answering some questions. Unfortunately, the sheriff's office cannot supply these records. All department case files from the 1940s, '50s, and early '60s "may have been archived somewhere."[27] No one knows their current whereabouts. Former sheriff's officer Myron Teegarden suspects that "a one-term sheriff we elected back in the sixties may have decided to clean house."[28] Regrettably, all reports filed by Denver police detectives assisting with the case were also turned over to the sheriff's office and suffered the same fate.

Great-nephew Russell Griffith told Yale Huffman in 1988, "Our family has numerous questions about the tragedy. Fred Lundy was a close friend of my parents, and there were many unanswered questions at the time. We think that Fred's death was classified as suicide out of administrative convenience rather than tangible proof."

Russell concluded, "It would be a tragic injustice if history blames him rather than the guilty, if that is the case."[29]

12

Ripples

The pavement at 13th and Welton radiated 98-degree heat at 2:00 in the afternoon of Monday, July 14, 2003. Nearly 150 people—students in nursing uniforms or chef's jackets or mechanics overalls, students with homemade noisemakers from a dozen nations, teachers, staffers, and assorted well-wishers with party horns—suffered gladly the relentless sun, glancing periodically up the street with excited anticipation.

At quarter past the hour, their vigil ended as Essie Garrett and Tonya Ciarochi jogged into view. Wearing sunbonnets, pioneer garb, and weary smiles, the two women had pulled a wagon 310 miles across the prairie, enduring 100-degree temperatures and 70-mile-an-hour winds—all the way from Arnold, Nebraska, to this parking lot between buildings of the Emily Griffith Opportunity School (EGOS). Amid cheers and applause, toots and jangles, they completed their nine-day marathon. The fifty-seven-year-old ultrarunner (Garrett) and her co-runner had retraced the Griffith family's 1894 journey and raised more than $17,000 for tuition assistance.

Garrett, an Opportunity School staff member for more than two decades, is well-known in Colorado for having raised more than $1 million over the past seventeen years for numerous charities. Ciarochi is a concert pianist with a doctorate in music. Like Emily, the women came from humble beginnings and continue to live modestly, emulating Griffith's philosophy and accomplishments. Their "Plains to the Rockies" run was a fund-raiser, as well as a tribute to the school's founder. Supporters were asked to pledge any amount they could per mile of the run. Setting out from Arnold the day after the Fourth of July, the runners planned to average thirty-one miles per day, "and the last two days we will push harder."[1]

"In today's economy," explained the July 2003 *News of LoDo and Downtown Denver,* "EGOS is serving a much larger number of students needing financial assistance, with the need per student greater than in past years. The Emily Griffith Foundation has awarded over $120,000 in scholarships during the past year, and this run will make future scholarships possible."

Garrett, who oversees the EGOS Receiving Department, credited Griffith as her inspiration. "I'm just trying to keep Miss Emily's philosophy alive," she told a reporter at the end of her journey. "I love the school."[2]

————

Had she not been cremated, Emily Griffith might have rolled over in her grave in 1991 when Denver Public Schools declared that the Opportunity School must become more self-supporting. For the first time in its history, the school could not offer tuition-free instruction. Dr. Carolyn Brink, a retired administrator who served the school for fifteen years, remembers that staff faced the decision with a mixture of fear for the school's survival and "disappointment that a piece of Emily's dream had eroded."

"I think Emily would have fought the move with all her heart and would probably have been successful since she was so well-connected in the community," Brink believes. Charging Denver residents for Opportunity classes put them on more equal footing with out-of-Denver students who had previously been assessed minimal fees. According to Dr. Brink's research, "Over the course of the years since tuition has been charged, the EGOS student population has changed significantly, with many more students who live outside of Denver attending."[3]

The school still offers the most affordable adult education in the state, and the Emily Griffith Foundation provides scholarship funds to those for whom even the minimal charges are prohibitive.

On June 18, 1947, just a few hours before Griffith's tragic death, Denver Public Schools authorized immediate construction of a new half-million-dollar expansion to the Opportunity School. When the four-story addition to Opportunity School opened in December 1949, students and visitors viewed a new plaque honoring the institution's founder. Jessie Ford Hansen, a shorthand teacher at the school since its beginning, headed the committee that raised money from teachers and staff who had served the school during its thirty-three years of operation. The memorial, designed and cast by J. E. Bullock of Denver, features a bas-relief portrait of Miss Emily. The inscription says simply, "Founder, Opportunity School. Principal 1916-1933." The dedication read at the plaque's unveiling described it as "a tribute not to Emily Griffith as a personality, but to Emily Griffith as the inspiration and guiding spirit of this school."[4]

The spirit and wisdom of Opportunity's leaders and their genius for adjustment continued to stand them in good stead throughout the succeeding decades. Course offerings responded to—or even anticipated—local employment trends. The many government and military agencies that moved into the area during the 1950s found plenty of well-prepared clerical workers among the school's Business and Office Skills graduates. As Denver hospitals and medical centers expanded, Opportunity trained more qualified medical technicians and licensed practical nurses.

Before the first passenger plane ever touched down at Stapleton Airport, EGOS students were studying jet engine repair. In the 1960s, Opportunity offered some of the first computer classes in the area in anticipation of Colorado's technology boom.

Nearly one-and-a-half million students have passed through Denver's Opportunity School. In the 2004–2005 academic year, EGOS served some 11,500 students and offered more than 350 day, evening, and weekend courses in 52 programs, making it the largest and most comprehensive adult training institution in the state.[5] The school covers an entire city block at its original 13th and Welton location. A walk past every shop and classroom takes more than one hour and covers more than a mile.

Emily would be astonished—and no doubt impressed—with the

school's Web site at www.egos-school.com. Here the visitor can find the most recent course catalog, with schedules and fees and information on how to get started as an EGOS student. In addition to a history section, current photos of students in classes can be accessed, along with valuable resource and career services sections that are updated regularly.

Sharon Robinson proudly served as the thirteenth lead administrator (principal) of the Emily Griffith Opportunity School until her August 2004 retirement. She taught business and marketing classes, areas in which Emily would have felt right at home. Robinson summed up her feelings about the school and Miss Emily.

> We still strive to meet the job-training needs of the under-served, house the largest English-as-a-Second-Language program for adults in Colorado, and have expanded our offerings to provide post-secondary technical training for business/industry in the State of Colorado. As the leading non-profit provider of post-secondary job training in the Greater Metro Denver area, EGOS provides a service not met by proprietary schools in that our tuition and fees are markedly lower, and our credit hours transfer to the community college system. We instill the self-confidence in students to continue with their higher education aspirations by removing the intimidation that "college" often presents to under-served populations.
>
> In completing my Masters studies in the mid-1980s, Emily Griffith Opportunity School was one of the featured topics of reading/discussion. Having the privilege and honor of serving as the school's Executive Director for four years was the furthest thing from my dreams at that time. It has truly been the most rewarding and exciting experience of my career in vocational edu-cation—to be associated with the history and tradition of Emily Griffith Opportunity School.[6]

Robinson's successor and current executive director of the school, Les Lindauer, is himself an EGOS alumnus. From 1971 through 1974, he attended Opportunity one night a week to learn welding in the Iron Workers Apprenticeship program. Lindauer points proudly to the fact that the Opportunity School consistently outperforms the state's community colleges in completion and job placement rates. He believes Miss Emily "would be proud of the amount of actual dollars percentage-wise that go directly to the classroom compared to our peers. She would be happy about the amount of 'public purpose' that this institution represents.

"I think she would be dismayed that [EGOS] is often looked down upon by higher education as 'that vocational school for dropouts,' which is not true."[7] Lindauer is quick to emphasize, however, that he feels Emily would focus only on the positives.

The foreign-born still find help and kindness at Emily Griffith. The school works with the Colorado Refugee English as a Second Language program to provide classes or in-home tutoring for refugees newly arrived from Bosnia, Somalia, Ethiopia, Sudan, Iraq, Iran, Burma, Vietnam, Russia, the Ukraine, and other countries. Professional ESL teachers are assisted by trained volunteers.

"I'm making a difference for two families while learning about their culture, their foods (delicious!), and their language," said ESL volunteer Lisa Voelz. "But the rewards go even deeper. Their positive attitude, sense of humor, and hope for the future—in spite of their disappointments, hardships, and continuing struggles—have taught me so much about the human spirit and have given me a better appreciation for life."[8]

Historian Tom "Dr. Colorado" Noel wrote in the *Denver Post Empire* Sunday magazine, "Nowadays, when immigrants are once again flooding into Colorado—and again encountering discrimination—Emily's story is instructive."[9]

The former soup kitchen in Opportunity's basement is now "Emily's Bistro," run by students in the Commercial Cooking, Baking, and Restaurant training programs. Students, staff, and community members can dine on excellent homemade soups, sandwiches, or daily specials for under $4, and purchase delicious baked goods to go. The cordial service comes with an appreciative smile.

Number 9 Pearl Street evolved over the years into the Emily Griffith Center, a residential treatment center for emotionally disturbed youth. As demand grew, the Home for Boys moved to a new Cheeseman Park location at 1260 Franklin. Soon, the needs of its temporary residents began to change, too. A home and a helping hand were no longer enough, as drugs, alcohol, gangs, sexual abuse, and neglect became the challenges. Every day, more boys were referred to treatment programs after enduring abuses and conditions every bit equal to the appalling circumstances Judge Lindsey exposed in *The Beast* to establish Denver's juvenile court system.

In 1980, the Emily Griffith Center moved to a beautiful rural location in the foothills outside of Larkspur, Colorado. It offers a chance for boys who have been in and out of foster and rehabilitation homes with no improvement. They may have had problems with school, with the law, or with substance abuse. In a ranchlike setting, the center's therapeutic program incorporates equine and wilderness therapies, along with the special education the troubled young men need. An associated treatment center in nearby Colorado Springs has recently grown to include day treatment and independent living programs, and the umbrella organizations are now called the Griffith Centers for Children.

"The children in treatment today at the Griffith Centers are entering our program more emotionally troubled than ever before," the center's Web site explains. "Today, we still strive to instill Emily's values into these children. The Griffith Centers teach [them] the skills to forgive and rebuild their lives with their families. We teach them how to love and trust again and to look forward to a better future."[10]

At least one of Emily's former students never got over his crush on the teacher. Alfred P. Adamo, an Italian immigrant who rose from janitor to head of a major Detroit real estate firm, considered Miss Griffith "an angel from heaven." For years after her retirement, Adamo sent her dolls, which she in turn donated to charity. One of the largest floral arrangements at the Griffith sisters' funeral was from Adamo and his wife.

When the Opportunity School was rededicated in December 1949, a tribute to Emily was held in Denver City Auditorium. Many suggestions were proposed for a fitting memorial to the educator, and Adamo offered $500 to be used toward a commemorative drinking fountain. Newspaper columnists shot down his idea, insisting that Opportunity itself was her memorial, and that an enlargement to the library, additional equipment, or scholarships in Griffith's name would be more appropriate. Undaunted, Adamo persisted.

On June 19, 1954, a black granite drinking fountain in Denver's Civic Center Park was dedicated to the memory of his friend and inspiration. The plaque reads:

> In memory of Emily Griffith, founder of Opportunity School. Devoted her life to her work as an educator, and through her energy, ambition and ability, built one of the greatest free adult industrial and vocational schools in the country, giving both young and old an opportunity to learn, develop their character, and become better citizens.[11]

For years, Adamo placed a single rose in memory of his "greatest treasure" every June on the anniversary of Miss Emily's passing.

The building erected in 1956 at the corner of 13th and Welton, site of the original Opportunity School, had the words from Emily's uncle's floating night school inscribed in stone at the top of the east-facing wall: "For All Who Wish to Learn." That same year, Jeanne Seckman of the Denver Public Schools solicited personal items of Emily's for a special room planned for the new building. "Miss Emily's Room" remains a favorite spot for meetings and special events. Display cases hold photographs, old class rosters, grade books and scrapbooks. Emily's Bible is there, with her name embossed on the cover in gold. So is a formal gown, white with gold embroidered starburst designs. She wore it in Omaha, Nebraska, on November 26, 1939, when honored as Woman of the Week on a radio program where, of course, no one could see it!

Certainly the stuff of drama, Emily's story has inspired at least two plays. A. Helen Anderson of Denver Public Schools wrote her script for the "Our American Schools" series. It was presented on March 30, 1938, and is generously quoted in Elinor Bluemel's biography of Griffith. A 1963 play about Emily Griffith was co-written by Bluemel and actress Maude Fealey. Fealey, playing the lead, headed a cast of thirty-nine. Tickets cost $2.50, and the local production ran September 16–27 at the Bonfils Theatre. Fittingly, the premiere benefited Denver Educational Senior Citizens.

In observance of the state's 1976 centennial celebration, the state legislature decided to add two stained glass windows to the capitol, commemorating outstanding Colorado women. Hundreds of letters poured in from Opportunity School graduates advocating its founder for the honor. A similar campaign had been mounted years earlier endorsing Griffith to represent Colorado in the National Statuary Hall, an honor that went instead to Dr. Florence Sabin in 1959. Emily was, however, selected for one of the centennial windows. Her portrait was hung in the senate chambers on the far left, balanced by the depiction of Virginia Neal Blue, the first woman to hold statewide office, on the far right.

In 1985, Emily's window was slated to be ousted from the senate to make way for a new stained glass portrait honoring Ruth Stockton, who had served twenty-four years as a state legislator. Emily's supporters were up in arms. Why should Griffith's window be the one to go? Why not Samuel Nicholson or Charles Hughes? How many lives had they changed for the better? "She [Griffith]...really didn't have anything to do with government," Senator Claire Traylor said to explain removing Emily's portrait.[12]

In the end, Senator Ruth Stockton, herself an Opportunity alumna (where she'd learned to type), insisted Miss Griffith's window be hung where it could still be seen from the senate chambers. She got her wish. Anyone standing at the second-floor entrance to the south-wing chambers need only turn around and gaze straight across the capitol's vast open interior to see the portrait of Emily, demure and serene-looking in a magnificent hat and elbow-length gloves, gazing back from her new, even more prominent position outside the former state supreme court chambers.

Upon the rededication of the window in its new location, a resolution by the state legislature and proclamation of Governor Richard Lamm declared the date—February 10, 1986—to be the 106th birthday of Miss Emily Griffith, thus making the 1880 birthdate that she gave Denver Public Schools so many years before, official. Surely she smiled down upon the proceedings.

Griffith is also included among the Colorado women depicted on the "Women's Gold" appliquéd wall hanging displayed on the first floor of the state capitol. The nine-by-twelve-foot wall hanging was the brainchild of Eve Mackintosh, who saw that the 1976 state centennial was an ideal time to highlight the civilizing influence of women whose faith in the future helped to shape the character of Colorado.

The women honored in hand-stitched embroidery and appliqué on linen were selected from a list suggested by Geraldine Merrill, historian for the committee that conceived the wall hanging. Miss Emily is portrayed holding a book and standing before a classic red schoolhouse. She is in good company. Among others featured on the piece are Denverites Mary Elitch Long (founder of the famous gardens and theater), Frances Wisehart Jacobs (the "Mother of Charities"), Mary Coyle Chase (Pulitzer Prize–winning author of the play *Harvey*), Agnes Reid Tammen (benefactor of Denver's Children's Hospital), and Mother Francesca Cabrini (America's first saint).

The Colorado Women's Hall of Fame recognized Emily as one of its inaugural inductees in 1985. Concerned that historical and contemporary women were not receiving appropriate acknowledgment for their foresight, vision, and pioneering accomplishments, the organization was created "to inspire by celebrating and sharing the lifetime contributions of Colorado's extraordinary women."[13]

In 1992, Emily was named to the "Colorado 100" list of distinguished citizens by the *Denver Post*, the Brown Palace, and Historic Denver, Inc. Sixty-eight years after the *Denver Post* first bestowed the title, Denver's Mayor Wellington Webb designated Emily Griffith the recipient of his Millennium Award for "Most Useful Citizen."

Useful. That was the ultimate compliment and the bottom line in Griffith's book. She found joy in purposeful pursuit. Never mind about her vision, her dedication to a dream for others, her humanity, or her courage. Ultimately, it is what you *do* with your life that ought to count, she insisted.[14]

———

Nearly sixty years after the Griffith sisters' tragic deaths, the cabin of devoted friend Fred Lundy still nestles alongside South Boulder Creek outside Pinecliffe, boarded up but little changed from the way he left it in June 1947. Emily and Florence's cabin is unrecognizable, enveloped by a newer, larger wooden home.

Ethelyn and Evans Gurtner shared the byline on a *Rocky Mountain News* Sunday magazine feature story published January 9, 1949, about Number 9 Pearl Street. On March 3—less than two years after her sisters' murders—Ethelyn died suddenly in Galveston, Texas, while vacationing with her husband.[15] In a letter from attorney Charles Blake to Evans dated December 1, 1949, Blake responded to concerns apparently expressed in Gurtner's previous correspondence that he was "not able at this time to close Ethel's estate" and had "not been feeling well and have had financial difficulties."[16]

The childless Gurtners sold nearly everything they owned not long after the deaths of Emily and Florence and traveled extensively. They had a particular fondness for cruises, which might explain how they came to be in Galveston during Ethel's final days.

An investigation of interment records reveals that Ethelyn Griffith Gurtner is buried in the plot adjacent to Emily and Florence's in Fairmount Cemetery. Evans never marked it with a headstone.

Griffith family members recall that Evans married again soon after Ethel's death to a woman with a small nest egg from her late husband's life insurance. Ethel's first successor passed away suddenly, of no apparent illness, a few years later.[17]

Evans married Nellie Powell in 1959 and settled in north Denver. He held a variety of jobs, as a steelworker, sewage plant worker, real estate broker, surveyor, and even shipbuilder. Despite repeated urgings to recount his memories of Emily and Florence Griffith's murders for the historical record, Evans Gurtner refused throughout his long life to talk about the incident or the circumstances surrounding it. "I was a secretary, and I offered to type it up," relative Phyllis Stevens recalled, "but he didn't want to go into it."[18] He died in 1980, taking whatever secrets he might have had to his grave.

––––––

Denver and the world have changed substantially since 1916. The priorities of everyday life have shifted, but human nature remains the same. The doors opened by universally accessible practical education are as essential to a community's economic and moral health now as they were then. The welfare-to-work and fast-track vocational training programs developed in response to 1990s welfare reforms and the introduction of Temporary Aid to Needy Families would be nothing new to Griffith. Her clarion call for public investment in human potential and workforce development resonates in national and international adult education policies to this day.

As part of President Lyndon Johnson's "Great Society" program, the Adult Education Act was created in 1966 with the aim of alleviating poverty by helping poorly educated adults earn a high school diploma. In the ensuing years, the act has broadened from requiring a basic secondary educational competency program to now encompassing work preparation, citizenship, and life skills. A 2000 report on future directions for adult education noted that recent trends have included "growth in intergovernmental and private sector collaborations…partnerships with employers, labor unions, public schools, community action organizations and…have expanded the purpose and outcomes of adult education beyond the traditional GED and ESL functions."[19] Emily Griffith's Opportunity School has done all these things and more, for more than eighty years.

President Bill Clinton had a vision for adult, minority, immigrant, and vocational education that was much like Griffith's. During his administration, he set forth a series of vocational retraining initiatives for citizens whose jobs had become obsolete or downsized. Clinton recognized the growing income gap among American workers as a product of the skills gap he sought to close. He proposed and fought for major funding for literacy initiatives and "universal re-employment" job training and career services. In 2000, Clinton enacted the largest investment in education in thirty years, part of which was allocated to help individuals limited in English proficiency with "civics and life skills instruction, including understanding the U.S. government system, the public education system, the workplace, and other key institutions of American life."[20] What sounded like innovation to most of the country was just another déjà vu for Denver's Opportunity School.

Echoes of Emily and her faculty meetings were unmistakable in President Clinton's message to UNESCO's 1997 Fifth International Conference on Adult Education in Hamburg, Germany. "Perhaps our most important pursuit as members of a global community is ensuring that all our citizens receive the education they need to make the most of their lives...Adult education provides crucial help for people seeking to lead productive and fulfilling lives, and I applaud each of you for your dedication to breaking down barriers and building new bridges to encourage lifelong learning."[21]

All people need compassion, consideration, and, above all, hope. It is simple, but it has never been easy. In times of discouragement or frustration, Emily recalled the heartening observation of an older woman, a student of Opportunity, who once reminded her, "There's all tomorrow that ain't been touched yet."[22]

Emily Griffith's death left many questions unanswered, but there is no question about her legacy. As long as there is a window in the state-house and a fountain in the park, she will be remembered. As long as there is an Opportunity School and a treatment center for troubled youth, her work will continue. And as long as teachers, counselors, staff and volunteers dedicate themselves to assisting others toward a better living and a better life, Miss Emily's spirit will continue to touch tomorrows.

Timeline

1868	Emily K. Griffith is born, eldest daughter of Andrew and Martha
1884	Emily graduates from the eighth grade, the highest level of formal education she will ever complete; Griffith family moves to Nebraska to homestead in Custer County; Emily teaches in one-room prairie schoolhouses and boards with students' families
1894	Griffith family moves to Denver
1895	Emily Griffith applies to Denver Public Schools; teaches as an alternate pending completion of training at Denver Normal School
1896–1904	Emily earns full teaching status; teaches sixth, seventh, and eighth grades at Central School in one of Denver's poorest neighborhoods
1904–1908	Emily serves as deputy state superintendent of schools
1908–1910	Emily returns to classroom teaching
1909	Emily is awarded a complimentary state teaching diploma
1910–1912	Emily serves as deputy state superintendent of public instruction
1911	Colorado State Teacher's College (now University of Northern Colorado) awards Emily an honorary pedagogy degree
1914	Emily teaches eighth grade at Twenty-fourth Street School in Denver's Five Points neighborhood and begins offering evening classes for adults and working children
1916	May 11, Board of Denver Public Schools authorizes Opportunity School and appoints Emily Griffith principal
	September 9, Opportunity School opens; more than 1,400 enroll the first week
1920	Emily is appointed to the State Child Welfare Board; Denver Kiwanis Club names her the first honorary female member
1922	Emily serves as president of the Colorado Education Association
1926	Opportunity School is expanded at 12th and Welton

1927	Emily and Denver Kiwanis Club help to establish Number 9 Pearl Street as a home for wayward boys (today's Griffith Centers for Children); University of Colorado awards Emily an honorary master of education degree
1932	Business and Professional Women of Denver names Emily 'Woman of the Year'
1933	Emily retires as principal of Opportunity School and moves to Pinecliffe with her sister, Florence
1933–1945	Emily serves on the State Board of Vocational Education
1934	Denver Board of Education adds Emily Griffith's name to Opportunity School in her honor
1942	Colorado Women's College awards Emily an honorary diploma in humanities
1947	June 18, Emily Griffith and her sister are slain in their Pinecliffe cabin
	In August, Fred Lundy's body is found in South Boulder Creek. Local authorities close the unsolved murder case
1956	Old Longfellow School building is razed; new building constructed at 13th and Welton
1972	Emily Griffith Opportunity School registers its one millionth student
1976	Emily Griffith is one of two women honored with a stained glass portrait window in the Colorado State Capitol; she is also featured on the "Women's Gold" tapestry created for Colorado's centennial
1980	Colorado Governor Richard Lamm proclaims February 10 Emily Griffith Day when her window is relocated and rededicated in the capitol
1985	Emily Griffith is named one the inaugural inductees in the Colorado Women's Hall of Fame
2000	Mayor Wellington Webb names Emily Griffith Denver's Most Useful Citizen in bestowing his Millennium Award

Endnotes

1 Headwaters

[1] Elinor Bluemel, *Emily Griffith and the Opportunity School of Denver* (Denver: by the author, 1954), 6.

[2] Yale Huffman, *The Life and Death of Emily Griffith* (Denver: by the author, 1989), 3.

[3] *In Memoriam,* Martha Craig Griffith, Manuscript File #1514, Stephen H. Hart Library, Colorado Historical Society, Denver.

[4] Bluemel, *Emily Griffith,* 6,7.

[5] Isabel Dodge Cornish, *A Pioneer Teacher Reminisces, in Pioneer Stories of Custer County* (1936), in Huffman, *Life and Death,* 7.

[6] Bluemel, *Emily Griffith.*

[7] "Literacy from 1870 to 1979: Educational Attainment and Illiteracy," National Center for Educational Statistics, http://nces.ed.gov/naa/historicaldata/edattain.asp accessed March 2, 2005.

[8] Yale Huffman, "Prairie Pluck: The Mission of Emily Griffith," *Sunday World Herald Magazine for the Midlands,* February 21, 1988.

[9] Yale Huffman, *Life and Death,* 10.

2 Confluence

[1] Yale Huffman, *Life and Death,* 12.

[2] Ibid., 11.

[3] Ibid., 12.

[4] Bluemel, *Emily Griffith,* 16.

[5] Alferd P. Adamo, Tribute Brochure, September 9, 1966, Clippings File, Denver Public Library, Western History Department.

[6] Mark Stuart, "Miss Opportunity," *Rocky Mountain News,* November 2, 1996, 24.

[7] Margaret Coel, *The Pride of Our People: The Colorado State Capitol* (Denver: Colorado General Assembly, 1992), 3–13.

[8] Bluemel, *Emily Griffith,* 14.

3 With the Flow

[1] "History of the 'Executive Residence,'" *Colorado State Archives* Web site, accessed October 22, 2002, available from http://archives.state.co.us/residence.html. Some poetic license is taken by placing Emily Griffith in the Cheesman home. Although there is no record of Emily ever visiting the Cheesman home, it is the sort of upper-class residence where she would have spoken to ladies clubs about her ideas for Opportunity School.

[2] Elinor Bluemel, *Emily Griffith and the Opportunity School of Denver* (Denver: by the author, 1954), 22.

[3] "Manual High School: History," Denver Public Schools Web site, accessed August 23, 2003, available from http://manual.dpsk12.org/history.html.

[4] Paul Essert, Foreword to *Opportunity School and Emily Griffith Its Founder,* by Elinor Bluemel (Denver: Green Mountain Press, 1970), xii.

4 Spring Thaw

[1] Frances Wayne, "My Memories of Emily Griffith," *Rocky Mountain News,* June 20, 1947.

[2] "Opportunity School" and "Frances Wayne" subject card files, *Denver Post* library. Denver, Colorado. The author scanned all issues of the *Denver Post* on microfilm from November 15, 1915 to May 11, 1916. She found no reference to Emily Griffith or her Opportunity School idea.

[3] Corinne Hunt, "She Didn't Waste Time on Tears," *Women Who Made the Headlines: Denver Women's Press Club—the First Hundred Years,* Cle Cervi and Nancy M. Peterson, eds. (Denver: Kimco, 1998), 35-36.

[4] Wayne, "My Memories."

5 From Trickle to Stream

1 Marie La Due, "New 'Opportutity School' to Teach Business to Pupils," *Denver Post*, May 12, 1916.

2 *Ibid.*

3 Bluemel, *Emily Griffith*, 29.

4 Elinor Bluemel, *Emily Griffith and the Opportunity School of Denver* (Denver: by the author, 1954), 75 (quoting a speech to the NEA, Seattle, Washington, 1927).

5 William E. Barrett, " Emily Griffith: Gift of a Sod Hut," *Rocky Mountain News*, May 20, 1962.

6 Bluemel, *Emily Griffith*, 33.

7 *Ibid.*, 46.

8 *Ibid.*, 34.

9 *Ibid.*

10 Clipping, Dawson Scrapbook Collection, Stephen H. Hart Library, Colorado Historical Society, Denver, Colorado.

11 Frances Wayne, "Every Stenographer in Denver Is Given Splendid Opportunity," *Denver Post*, September 4, 1919, 13.

12 Bluemel, *Emily Griffith*, 34.

13 *Ibid.*, 22.

14 Thomas Aquinas, Sum Theol. I-II, q.57, a.5. Quoted in Matthew Fox, *The Reinvention of Work* (New York: Harper Collins, 1995), 1, 2.

15 The Gurtners' Colorado marriage license lists the age of the bride and groom as 26 and 24 respectively. This is consistent with the 1891 year of birth cited in Ethel's obituary. It is contrary to the information uncovered by biographer Yale Huffman using the 1885 Nebraska State Census.

16 Suzanne Finck, Archives and Rare Books Department, University of Cincinnati, letter to the author, April 23, 2004.

17 "In Memoriam, Martha Craig Griffith," Manuscript File 1514, Stephen H. Hart Library, Colorado Historical Society, Denver, Colorado.

6 Against the Current

1 Robert A. Goldberg, "Denver: Queen City of the Colorado Realm," in *The Invisible Empire in the West*, Shawn Lay, ed. (Urbana and Chicago: University of Illinois Press, 1992), 39-63.

2 Robert A. Goldberg, *Hooded Empire: The Klu Klux Klan in Colorado* (Urbana and Chicago: University of Illinois Press, 1981), 10-11.

3 *Ibid.* 23.

4 *Ibid.* 24.

5 *Ibid.* 25.

6 Goldberg, *Invisible Empire*, 44.

7 *Ibid.*

8 Goldberg, *Hooded Empire*, 73-78.

9 Carl Abbott, Stephen Leonard, and David McComb, *Colorado: A History of the Centennial State* (Boulder: Colorado Associated University Press, 1982, rev. ed.), 271.

10 Goldberg, *Hooded Empire*, 95-99.

11 "Federal Agents Scent Plot at Trade School," *Denver Post*, June 24, 1917.

12 Bluemel, *Emily Griffith*, 49.

13 Manuscript File 1514, Stephen H. Hart Library, Colorado Historical Society, Denver, Colorado.

7 New Channels

1 Elinor Bluemel, *Emily Griffith and the Opportunity School of Denver* (Denver: by the author, 1954), 74.

2 Emily Griffith Opportunity School Archives, Denver, Colorado.

3 Bluemel, *Emily Griffith*, 36.

4 "You Can Do It," *Time*, July 8, 1946.

5 Bluemel, *Emily Griffith* 36.

6 *Ibid.*

7 Emily Griffith, "She Helped Men Help Themselves," *Denver Post*, July 5, 1946,

8 Pearl S. Coberly, "Emily Griffith: An Appreciation," *The Colorado School Journal*, 49, no. 6 (February 1934).

[9] Dawson Scrapbooks, Vol. 42, Stephen H. Hart Library, Colorado Historical Society, Denver, Colorado.

[10] "Men Needn't Fear Women in Business, Club is Told," *Rocky Mountain News*, February 10, 1927.

[11] Bluemel, *Emily Griffith*, 20.

[12] *Ibid.*, 39.

[13] *Denver Post*, September 7, 1930, 19.

[14] Bluemel, *Emily Griffith*, 5.

[15] Frances Wayne, "Emily Griffith Alone Deserves Credit for Opportunity School," *Denver Post*, May 5, 1919, Sec. 1, 7.

[16] *Denver Post*, September 7, 1930, 19.

[17] *Fusion Facts,* July 1934, Emily Griffith Opportunity School Archives.

[18] *Denver Post*, September 7, 1930, 19.

[19] Bluemel, *Emily Griffith*, 20.

8 Tributaries

[1] Judge Charles Rosenbaum, "My Debt to Emily Griffith," *Rocky Mountain News Empire Magazine*, November 27, 1966, 12-13.

[2] Benjamin B. Lindsey, *The Beast* (Seattle: University of Washington Press, 1970). Original publication date 1910.

[3] *Ibid.*

[4] *Ibid.*

[5] Unpublished booklet dated July 17, 1943, Denver Kiwanis Club Archives.

[6] *Ibid.*

[7] Russell Griffith, telephone interview with the author, November 23, 2005.

[8] Ethel Gurtner and Evans J. Gurtner, "No. 9 Pearl," *Rocky Mountain News Empire Magazine*, January 9, 1949.

[9] "Kiwanis Objectives," Kiwanis International Web site, accessed July 30, 2003, available at http://www.kiwanis.org/aboutkiwanis.html.

[10] Letter from Paul Essert to Denver Kiwanis Club, June 15, 1946, Denver Kiwanis Club Archives.

[11] *Ibid.*

[12] Elinor Bluemel, *Emily Griffith and the Opportunity School of Denver* (Denver: by the author, 1954) 16.

9 Out of the Mainstream

[1] Ernie Pyle, "Opportunity School Spirit Wins Praise," syndicated newspaper column, October 1, 1936.

[2] Lee Casey, "Emily Griffith, Retired, is Teaching Again," *Rocky Mountain News*, November 6, 1945, 16.

[3] *Ibid.*

[4] Elinor Bluemel, *Emily Griffith and the Opportunity School of Denver* (Denver: by the author, 1954), 66.

[5] Casey, "Emily Griffith, Retired," 16.

[6] Unsigned letter, October 19, 1934, Emily Griffith Opportunity School Archives.

[7] Ernie Pyle, October 1, 1936.

[8] Jeanne Varnell, *Women of Consequence: The Colorado Women's Hall of Fame* (Boulder: Johnson Books, 1999), 76.

[9] Casey, "Emily Griffith, Retired," 16.

[10] *Ibid.*

[11] Correspondence, Denver Kiwanis Club Archives.

[12] Bluemel, *Emily Griffith*, 68.

[13] Correspondence, Denver Kiwanis Club Archives.

[14] "You Can Do It," *Time*, July 8, 1946.

[15] Denver Radio Station KOA sound recording, June 26, 1946. Emily Griffith Opportunity School Archives.

[16] Correspondence, Denver Kiwanis Club Archives.

10 Troubled Waters

[1] Photo caption. *Denver Post,* June 21, 1947 (Floyd McCall, photographer).

[2] "Friends Grieved by Tragic Death," *Denver Post,* June 21, 1947.

[3] *Ibid.*

[4] "Few People Knew About Emily's Sister Florence," *Denver Post,* June 19, 1947, 1.

[5] "Griffith 'Mercy' Motive Studied," *Rocky Mountain News*, June 20, 1947, 5.

[6] *Ibid.*

[7] Peter Chronis, "Doubts Linger After Griffith Murders," *Denver Post,* July 20, 1997, 13.

[8] Former Mayor Quigg Newton, telephone interview with the author, April 6, 2003.

[9] "Friends Grieved by Tragic Death," *Denver Post,* June 21, 1947.

[10] Frances Wayne, "My Memories of Emily Griffith," *Rocky Mountain News,* June 20, 1947, 5.

[11] Phil J. Rodgers, "Griffith Death Comes as Shock to Capitol," *Denver Post,* June 26, 1947.

[12] Gene Lindberg, "Griffith Sisters' Rites Marked by Simplicity," *Denver Post,* June 22, 1947.

[13] Betty Caldwell, "Denver Pays Final Tribute Today to Emily Griffith, Doer of Good," *Rocky Mountain News,* June 22, 1947.

[14] Robert L. Perkin, "City Pays Tribute to Emily Griffith and Her Sister," *Rocky Mountain News,* June 22, 1947, 14.

[15] Arthur Baldwin, Eulogy for Emily Griffith, Denver Kiwanis Club Archives.

[16] Leslie Osgood, Historian, Central Presbyterian Church, Denver, Colorado. Undated note to the author.

11 Murky Depths

[1] Peter Chronis, "Doubts Linger After Griffith Murders," *Denver Post,* July 20, 1997, 13.

[2] "Famous Educator and Sister are Found Slain at Pinecliffe," *Boulder Daily Camera,* June 19, 1947.

[3] "How to Identify Lundy," *Boulder Daily Camera,* June 20, 1947.

[4] *Rocky Mountain News,* June 22, 1947.

[5] "Fugitive Warrant Opens Griffith Case to FBI," *Boulder Daily Camera,* June 22, 1947.

[6] D. Myron Teegarden, telephone interview with the author, September 14, 2003.

[7] "Mystery of Griffith Slayings Uncracked; Search Continues," *Boulder Daily Camera,* June 21, 1947.

[8] "Search for Lundy Continues in Area Around Pinecliffe," *Boulder Daily Camera,* July 3, 1947.

[9] Teegarden interview, September 14, 2003..

[10] "Murder in Pinecliffe," *Time,* June 30, 1947, 18.

[11] "Griffith 'Mercy' Motive Studied," *Rocky Mountain News,* June 20, 1947, 5.

[12] *Ibid.*

[13] "Police Order Recheck of Lundy Case," *Boulder Daily Camera,* June 20, 1947.

[14] "Lundy Letter to Brother...Revealed by Sheriff's Office," *Boulder Daily Camera,* June 26, 1947.

[15] Bernard Beckwith, "New Lundy Search Mystery," *Denver Post,* July 17, 1947, 1.

[16] "Skeleton of Leg...'Is This Fred Lundy?'," *Boulder Daily Camera,* June 26, 1947.

[17] "Emily Griffith's Will Admitted to Probate," *Boulder Daily Camera,* July 5, 1947.

[18] Thomas Meier, *Ed Tangen, The Pictureman* (Boulder: Boulder Creek Press, 1984).

[19] "Griffith Bullet Identified," *Denver Post,* June 21, 1947.

[20] "Anonymous Friend of Emily Griffith Offers $100 Reward for Finding Lundy," *Boulder Daily Camera,* July 3, 1947.

[21] "Two 'Clues' . . . Prove Valueless," *Boulder Daily Camera,* June 25, 1947.

[22] Chronis, "Doubts Linger," *Denver Post.*

[23] Steve Lipsher, "Ten Colorado Originals: Real People Who Made a Real Difference," *Denver Post,* December 31, 1999, 24A.

[24] Chronis, "Doubts Linger," *Denver Post.*

[25] Yale Huffman, telephone interview with the author, August 29, 2003.

[26] Teegarden interview, September 14, 2003.

[27] Corresponence from Lt. Joseph A. Gang, Boulder County Sheriff's Department, to the author, December 9, 2002.

[28] Teegarden interview, September 14, 2003.

[29] Yale Huffman, "Prairie Pluck: The Mission of Emily Griffith," *Sunday World Herald Magazine for the Midlands,* February 21, 1988.

12 Ripples

[1] "Runners Follow Historical Trail," *Arnold Sentinel* (Nebraska), July 10, 2003, 1, 2.

2 Susan Froyd, "Long Distance Runner Essie Garrett Pulls Ahead for Emily's Sake," *Westword*, July 14, 2003.

3 Carolyn Brink, e-mail to the author, December 17, 2003.

4 "Plaque at Opportunity School Honors Founder Emily Griffith," *Denver Post*, December 6, 1949.

5 Kari Gomez-Smith, public relations officer, EGOS, e-mail to author, May 19, 2005.

6 Sharon Robinson, e-mail to author, November 25, 2003.

7 Les Lindauer, e-mail to author, May 17, 2005.

8 "Lisa's Story," Colorado Refugees English as a Seond Language Program Web site, available at http://www.refugee-esl.org/story.html, accessed April 19, 2002.

9 Tom Noel, "Emily Griffith Opened Up World of Opportunity in Denver," *Denver Post Empire*, April 27, 1997, 5.

10 "History of Emily Griffith Center," Emily Griffith Web site, available at http://www.emilygriffith.com/history.html, accessed November 17, 2003.

11 Greg Pinney, "Tribute Paid Emily Griffith," *Denver Post*, January 11, 1976.

12 John Sanko, "Educator's Window in Senate Chamber Gets Boot," *Rocky Mountain News*, December 22, 1985.

13 Mission statement, Colorado Women's Hall of Fame. Denver: Colorado Women's Hall of Fame, 2002.

14 Elinor Bluemel, *Emily Griffith and the Opportunity School of Denver* (Denver: by the author, 1954).

15 Obituary, "Ethelyn Griffith Gurtner," *Rocky Mountain News*, March 13, 1949, 37.

16 Manuscript File 1514, Stephen H. Hart Library, Colorado Historical Society, Denver.

17 Russell Griffith, letter to Yale Huffman, April 25, 1988. Copy provided to the author by Sheri Griffith Lorbeck.

18 Phyllis Stevens, telephone interview with the author, June 1, 2005.

19 Thomas G. Stricht, "Beyond 2000. Future Directions for Adult Education," available at http://www.nald.ca/fulltext/beyond.htm, accessed December 18, 2003.

20 "President Clinton and Vice President Gore: Expanding Education Opportunities for Hispanic Americans," Office of the White House Press Secretary, National Archives and Records Administration Web site, available at http://clinton3.nara.gov/Wh/New/html/20000615.html, accessed December 18, 2003.

21 "Message from U.S. President Clinton to UNESCO's Conference on Adult Education in Hamburg," USESCOPRESS Web site, available at http://www.unesco.org/bpi/eng/cofintea/clinton.htm, accessed December 18, 2003.

21 Bluemel, *Emily Griffith*, 63.

Sources Consulted

Newspapers

Boulder Daily Camera
Commerce City Beacon
Denver Post
Douglas County News Press
North Denver Tribune
Rocky Mountain News
The Arnold Sentinel (NE)
Westword

Books

Abbott, Carl, Stephen J. Leonard, and David McComb. *Colorado: A History of the Centennial State,* Rev. Ed. Boulder: Colorado Associated University Press, 1982.

Biographic Dictionary of American Educators. Vol. 2. John F. Ohles, editor, Westport, Connecticut: Greenwood Press, 1978.

Bluemel, Elinor. *Emily Griffith and the Opportunity School of Denver.* Boulder: by the author, 1954.

Bluemel, Elinor. *One-Hundred Years of Colorado Women.* Denver: by the author, 1973.

Bluemel, Elinor. *Opportunity School and Emily Griffith Its Founder.* Denver: Green Mountain Press, 1970.

Bluemel, Elinor. *The Golden Opportunity.* Boulder: Johnson Publishing Co., 1965.

Bueler, Gladys R. *Colorado's Colorful Characters.* Boulder: Pruett Publishing, 1981.

Coel, Margeret. *The Pride of Our People: The Colorado State Capitol.* Denver: Colorado General Assembly, 1992.

Dalquist, Dorothy. *Women's Gold.* Denver:

Colorado General Assembly, 1995.

Doenecke, Justus P. *The Presidencies of James A. Garfield and Chester A. Arthur.* Lawrence: The Regents Press of Kansas, 1981.

Fox, Matthew. *The Reinvention of Work: A New Vision of Livelihood for Our Time.* New York: Harper Collins Publishers, 1995.

Goldberg, Robert A, "Denver: Queen City of the Colorado Realm." In *The Invisible Empire in the West,* Shawn Lay, ed. Urbana: University of Illinois Press, 1992.

Goldberg, Robert Alan. *Hooded Empire: The Ku Klux Klan in Colorado.* Urbana: University of Illinois Press, 1981.

Goodstein, Phil. *The Ghosts of Denver: Capitol Hill.* Denver: New Social Publications, 1996.

Hosokawa, William. *Thunder in the Rockies: The Incredible Denver Post.* New York: William Morrow & Co., 1976.

Huffman, Yale. *The Life and Death of Emily Griffith.* Denver: Westerner's Roundup, 1989.

Hunt, Corrine, "She Didn't Waste Time on Tears," in *The Women Who Made the Headlines: Denver Women's Press Club - The First Hundred Years.* Cle Cervi and Nancy M. Peterson, eds. Lakewood, CO: Western Guideways, 1998.

Leonard, Stephen J. and Thomas J. Noel. *Denver: Mining Camp to Metropolis.* Niwot: University Press of Colorado, 1990.

Lindsey, Benjamin B. *The Beast.* Seattle: University of Washington Press, 1970.

Mauck, Laura M. *Five Points Neighborhood of Denver.* Chicago: Arcadia Publishing, 2001.

McKeever, Gene, Kenyon Forrest, and Raymond McAllister. *History of the Public Schools of Denver.* Denver: Tramway Press, 1989.

Meier, Thomas J. *Ed Tangen, The Pictureman.* Boulder: Boulder Creek Press, 1994.

Noel, Thomas J. with Stephen J. Leonard and Kevin E. Rucker. *Colorado Givers: A History of Philanthropic Heroes.* Niwot: University Press of Colorado, 1998.

Notable American Women: 1607-1950. Edward T. James, Editor. Cambridge, MA: Belknap Press of Harvard University Press, 1971.

Schneider, Dorothy and Carl J. Schneider. *American Women in the Progressive Era, 1900-1920.* New York: Facts on File, 1993.

Varnell, Jeanne. *Women of Consequence: The Colorado Women's Hall of Fame.* Boulder: Johnson Books, 1999.

Wenger, George R. *The Story of Mesa Verde National Park.* Mesa Verde Museum Association, Inc., 1991.

Articles

Baldwin, Arthur. "Eulogy for Emily Griffith." *The Denver Kiwanian* (July 2, 1947).

Coberly, Pearl S. "Emily Griffith: An Appreciation." *Colorado School Journal* (April 1934).

Cohen, Ruth. "Emily Griffith's Dream Come True:New Building to be Dedicated." *The Monitor* (December 2, 1949).

"Emily Speeds Up on the Information Highway." *Welton Street Journal,* Vol. XXVII, no.1 (October 2001).

Haines, Florence Wilson. "Interesting Personalities in P.E.O." *The P.E.O. Record* (December 1929).

Halaas, David Fridjtjof. "Emily Griffith: Let Me Tell You of a Hope." *Colorado History NOW* (June 1999).

Huffman, Yale. "Prairie Pluck: The Mission of Emily Griffith." *Sunday World Herald Magazine of the Midlands* (February 21, 1988).

Kostka, Dorothy. "Emily's Pupils: The Strength of a City." *Reader's Digest* (September 1963).

"Murder in Pinecliffe." *Time* (June 30, 1947).

Noel, Thomas. "Emily Griffith Opened Up World of Opportunity in Denver." *Rocky Mountain News Empire* (April 27, 1997).

"Opportunity Always Knocks Twice." *Fortune Magazine* (November 1939).

Pyle, Ernie. "Opportunity School Spirit Wins Praise." Syndicated column (October 1, 1936).

Rosenbaum, Charles. "My Debt to Emily Griffith." *Rocky Mountain News Empire* (November 27, 1966).

Smith, Ellison. "A Tribute to Miss Emily." *Denver Post Roundup* (September 16, 1963).

"The Opportunity School of Denver." *Fusion Facts* (July 1934).

"You Can Do It." *Time* (July 8, 1946)

Zahller, Alissa. "Curator's Corner: The Clio Club." *Colorado History NOW* (August 2003).

Pamphlets

Adamo, Alfred. *"A Tribute to Emily Griffith."* Denver Public Library Western History Department clippings file, "Emily Griffith."

Chester, Christie M. "Emily Griffith Boys' Home, Inc. – The Name Isn't All That's Changed." (1977).

Colorado Women's Hall of Fame Induction 2002 Program.

Emily Griffith Opportunity School. Colorado Historical Society clippings file, "Emily Griffith."

"Emily Griffith Opportunity School – 50th Anniversary." Denver Public Schools (1966).

"No. 9 Pearl Street." The Denver Foundation (1933).

Stevenson, Irene and others. "Emily Griffith." (July 17, 1943).

Archival Materials

Central Presbyterian Church Archives, Denver.

Colorado Chapter E, P.E.O. Sisterhood. Archival Files.

Colorado State Archives.

Denver Kiwanis Club. Archival Files.

Denver Post Library, Subject Index Card Files.

Emily Griffith Opportunity School. Archival Files.

Emily Griffith. Manuscript File #1514, Stephen H. Hart Library, Colorado Historical Society. Processed by Meredith Dries, 1993; Collection donated by Williard and Patty Stephens (1992).

Interviews

Brink, Dr. Carolyn, former administrator EGOS, December 11, 2003.

Gomez-Smith, Kari, Public Relations officer for EGOS, interviewed by Debra Faulkner on numerous occasions, 2000-2003.

Griffith, Russell C., Emily Griffith's great-nephew, November 23, 2005.

Huffman, Yale, Emily Griffith biographer, August 28, 2003.

Lindauer, Les, Executive Director of EGOS, May 17, 2005.

Newton, Quigg, Mayor of Denver at time of Emily Griffith's murder, April 8, 2003.

Picena-White, Carmen, Public Relations officer for EGOS, interviewed 1999-2000.

Robinson, Sharon, Executive Director of EGOS, November 25, 2003.

Stevens, Phyllis, Gurtner relative, June 1, 2005.

World Wide Web

"A Family Treatment and Education Agency Established in 1927 by Miss Emily Griffith." Emily Griffith Center. *www.EmilyGriffith.com/Frame.html.*

"Colorado's Executive Residence." State of Colorado. *www.archives.state.co.us/residence.html.*

"History of the School." Emily Griffith Opportunity School. *www.egos-school.com/information/history/.*

"History: Emily Griffith Opportunity School."Denver Public Schools. *www.dpsk12.org/aboutdps/history/dps_history_griffith.shtml.*

"Manual's History." Manual High School. *http://manual.denver.k12.co.us/history.html.*

"Message from U.S. President Clinton to UNESCO's Conference on Adult Education in Hamburg." UNESCO.

www.unesco.org/bpi/eng/confintea/clinton.htm.

"President Clinton and Vice President Gore: Expanding Education Opportunities for Hispanic Americans." Office of the White House Press Secretary. National Archives and Records Administration. *http://clinton3.nara.gov/WH/New/html/20000615.html.*

"Remarks by the President on Closing the Skills Gap." Office of the White House Press Secretary. University of North Texas-Dallas. *http://govinfo.library.unt.edu/npr/library/speeches/012899.html.*

"Serving the Children of the World: Kiwanis International." Kiwanis International. *www.kiwanis.org/.*

Sticht, Thomas G., "Beyond 2000: Future Directions for Adult Education." National Adult Literacy Database. *www.nald.ca/fulltext/beyond/toc.htm.*

Weber, Brian. "Griffith Answered When Opportunity Knocked." *Rocky Mountain News* website. *www.denver-rmn.com/millennium/.*

Other Sources

"About Central Church." Informational flyer published by Central Presbyterian Church, Denver.

Adamo, Alfred P. Dedication Speech for Emily Griffith Memorial Fountain. (June 18, 1954).

Cline, Effie M. Opportunity School class roster (June 1919).

Colorado Executive Order # 000094. Legislative Services Library, Colorado State Capitol.

Dawson Scrapbooks, Vol. 42, pp.42-45. Stephen H. Hart Library, Colorado Historical Society, Denver.

Denver City Directories 1910-1935 (on microfilm). Stephen H. Hart Library, Colorado Historical Society, Denver.

Emily Griffith's Speech to Denver Kiwanis Club, Audio Tape. Recorded by KOA Radio, EGOS Archives, (June 1946).

Fairmount Cemetery, Denver, Colorado. Interment Records (Block 61).

Gang, Lt. Joseph A. Boulder County Sheriff's Department. Letter to Debra Faulkner (December 9, 2002).

Griffith, Russell C., Letter to Yale Huffman (April 25, 1988).

Osgood, Leslie. Central Presbyterian Church Historian. Letter to Debra Faulkner (November 12, 2003).

Poster for Opportunity School registration, classes beginning September 9, 1936. Western History Department, Denver Public Library, clippings file, "Emily Griffith."

Seldon, Eugene G. Annual Report of the Superintendent, Denver Public Schools (1917). Colorado State Archives.

State of Colorado Marriage Licenses. Herbert Willis and Ethelyn Griffith, July 27, 1904; Evans J. Gurtner and Ethelyn R. Griffith, December 19, 1917; State of Colorado Divorce Decree: Herbert Willis and Ethelyn Willis, November 9, 1914; Evans J. Gurtner and Nellie A. Powell, August 15, 1959, (microfilm). Western History Department, Denver Public Library.

Index

Acknowledgments

Little did I imagine when I first donned a fancy hat to portray Miss Emily Griffith that it would lead to more than five years of historical detective work. Clues came from myriad sources, and like Emily, I have many people to thank for helping transform my dream into reality.

From the outset, the public relations office of the Emily Griffith Opportunity School graciously granted me access to anything and everything in the school archives. Carmen Picena-White and Kari Gomez-Smith could not have been more helpful and supportive, patiently answering all my inquiries. Frank Aguilar produced beautifully digitized versions of the photos and other images without a word of complaint about how numerous they were. Former and current EGOS executive directors Dr. Carolyn Brink, Sharon Robinson, and Les Lindauer all provided thoughtful and insightful twenty-first-century perspectives on Miss Emily and the school's legacy.

I am indebted to Carol Taylor, *Boulder Daily Camera* librarian, who photocopied the newspaper's entire clippings file on the murder, investigation and manhunt for Fred Lundy, enabling me to thoroughly document that part of Emily's story. Thanks to Dock Myron Teegarden, former Boulder County sheriff's officer, who kindly shared his recollections of the unsolved crime.

The helpful and ever-patient staff members of the Colorado Historical Society's Stephen H. Hart Library and of the Denver Public Library's Western History and Genealogy department offered expertise and knowledgeable assistance throughout the evolution of this book. *Denver Post* librarians Vicky Makings and Anne E. Feiler saved me untold hours of microfilm scanning, effectively narrowing my search for articles by reporter Frances Wayne.

I am grateful to Keith Schrum of the Colorado Historical Society for putting me in touch with Griffith manuscript donors Patti and Willard "Ike" Stevens. I appreciate their willingness, as well as that of Gurtner relative Phyllis Stevens, to fill in whatever blanks they could. Very special thanks are due also to Emily's great-grandnephew Russell Griffith and his daughter (Emily's great-great-grandniece), Sheri Griffith Lorbeck, for sharing family memories and insights.

Joyce Perkins of the *P.E.O. Record* and Evelyn Estes, archivist of the Colorado Chapter E; Don Anderson and Dave Webster of the Denver Kiwanis Club; Leslie Osgood of the Central Presbyterian Heritage Center; Ellen Metter of the Auraria Library; Edna Pelzmann of the Colorado State Capitol; and Renee Dees and Howard Shiffman of the Griffith Centers for Children all contributed important pieces to the processes of researching and crafting this book.

I particularly wish to thank fellow Griffith biographers Yale Huffman and Joyce Lohse for generously sharing their own experiences, discoveries, and enthusiasm for the subject. Special thanks are due my publisher, Doris Baker, who believed in the importance of updating Miss Emily's story.

Without the initial assignment and supportive guidance of Professor Tom Noel, this book would never have been completed. Gently but firmly, he made me stop researching, start writing, and keep persisting. For his unfailing encouragement and his mentorship, I am forever beholden.

When merely tolerating my obsession with Emily Griffith would have been heroic, my husband, James, went much further, supporting me—financially, logistically, and wholeheartedly—in the pursuit of her story and of my graduate degree. My gratitude and love for him are boundless.

Finally, I wish to thank all the people who have responded to my first-person portrayals of Miss Emily almost as if to the visionary educator herself, expressing their appreciation for the ways in which her Opportunity School touched their own lives or the lives of relatives or acquaintances. It is this outpouring of heartfelt gratitude that inspired me more than anything else to chronicle Emily Griffith's story as completely and as respectfully as possible.

About the Author

Debra Faulkner grew up in Loveland, Colorado. She earned her BS in Education from the University of Colorado and is currently pursuing a master's degree in history at the University of Colorado at Denver. She is a recent Anschutz fellow and longtime volunteer with the Colorado Historical Society. In addition to serving as editor of UCD's *Historical Studies Journal,* Debra is co-author of a history of Colorado with Professor Thomas J. Noel. As a Colorado Women's Hall of Fame board member, she manages the organization's archives and collects life stories of contemporary inductees for the ongoing oral history project.

Debra portrays Emily Griffith and other notable women from Colorado's past in first-person programs. She lives with her husband and their frenetic border collie on a lake north of Denver.